구상 — 초토의 시

Wasteland Poems
Poems of Ku Sang

Translated by Brother Anthony of Taizé

Wasteland Poems

Translated by Brother Anthony of Taizé

Original Poems © Ku Sang
Translation © 2000 Brother Anthony
First published as *Wastelands of Fire* by Forest Books(London) in 1990.
Published by DapGae Books
#201 Won Bld.
829-22 Bangbae 4-dong, Socho-ku, Seoul 137-064 Korea
Tel / (02) 532-4867, 591-8267, 537-0464, 596-0464   Fax / 594-0464

DapGae

English Translations
of Korean Literature Series

머리말

시인 구상具常은 1919년 9월 16일 대한민국 서울에서 태어났다. 당시 한국은 일본에 강점된 지 10년이 되던 해로 독립에의 강한 열망을 드러내기 시작하던 때였다. 그가 어린 시절부터 휘말려들게 된 극적인 사건과 고통들은 바로 근대 한국을 특징짓는 것이기도 했다. 그는 주로 언론계에서, 여론의 세계 속에 살아오면서 때로는 정치범으로 구속되기도 하고 대학 강단에 서기도 했다. 구상은 언론인, 주필, 해외특파원, 수필가, 극작가, 교수였으나 이런 모든 것에 앞서 그는 늘 시인이었다. 그는 가톨릭 문우회와 국제 펜클럽 한국지부 회장직을 역임했고 많은 문학상을 수상했고, 한국문단의 명사 중 하나로 아직도 많은 독자를 확보하고 있다.

1984년 구상은 『모과木瓜 옹두리에도 사연이』라는 일련의 작품을 발표했는데, 이 초기시들은 그의 어린 시절과 청년기의 성장과정을 묘사하고 있다. 이 가운데 첫 작품에서 그는 1920년대 초 자신의 가족이 어떻게 서울을 떠나 북한의 원산으로 이사가게 되었는지를 회상하고 있는데, 그에게는 원산이 아직도 진정한 고향으로 남아 있다. 한국적 정서에 친숙한 사람이라면 구상이 기억하고 있는 정서적 첫 경험이 눈물이라는 사실에 전혀 놀라지 않을 것이다.

그는 천주교 집안에서 태어났고 천주교 신부였던 그의 형님은 1950년 다른 사제들과 함께 북한에서 순교한 것으로 추정된다. 구상은 얼마간 소신학교小神學校에 다니다가 '도망'쳤고, 그 뒤 동경에서 일본대학 학생이 되어 서구의 온갖 급진사상, 특히 불란서의 급진사상을 접하게 된다. 종교철학을 공부하던 이 위기의 시절에 마침내 그에게 하나의 탈출구가 되어 준 것이 시였다. 구상은 학문을 통해 '여러 사상의 추종자'가 되어 귀국하여 1942년 지금은 북한이 되어 버린 지역에서 언론인으로 활동하게 된다. 몇년 뒤 그는 어머니를 포함한 가족을 남겨 둔 채 월남하는 처지에 놓이게 된다.

남쪽에서의 생활도 순탄치는 않아서, 한국 동란(1950~1953)이 끝난 후 권력의 부패상을 비판하는 『민주고발民主告發』이라는 정치평론을 발표했다가 감옥에 갇히게 된다. 구상은 옥고를 치르는 동안 얻은 폐결핵 때문에 폐에 구멍이 뚫렸다고 가끔 말하곤 한다.

1946년 남한으로 탈출하기 전, 그는 원산에서 첫 시집을 낸 바 있는데, 한국 동란의 경험은 1956년에 나온 『초토焦土의 시』에 기록되어 있다. 이 시집에서 우리는 한국의 분단을 기정사실로 받아들이기를 거부하는 민족 통일의 의지를 분명히 감지하게 되거니와, 이것이야말로 구상의 많은 시에 나타나는 뚜렷한 특징이기도 하다. 이들 전쟁시편의 중요한 특징이 있다면 모든 시적인 기교를 배격한 것이 그것이고, 여기서 시인은 복잡한 시적인 효과나 도덕적 설교를 동원하지 않고 풍경과 자연의 모습을 환기하여 보여 줄 뿐이다.

인생무상의 주제 또한 구상의 주요 주제 가운데 하나이며, 이것은 그의 이름과 관련된 말장난의 일부로 이루어지고 있다. 그의 이름인 '상'常이라는 글자는 '지속'과 '불변'을 뜻하는 한자로, 철학적으로는 가령 노자의 도덕경 첫 구절에 표현된 대로, 변하지 않는 실재의 추구의 일부를 이룬다. 특히 개인적인 내용을 담고 있는 '덧없는 나'라는 뜻의 「구상무상」이라는 일련의 시에서 한국어 제목의 '무'無는 '덧없음'이라는 낱말에서 '없음'에 해당한다. 구상은 현대 한국의 젊은 세대들이 이해하기 어려운 추상적이고 관념적인 의미로 가득 찬 한자를 사용함으로써 풍부한 의미와 암시를 만들어 내고 있으며 그로 인해 그 의미를 영어로 표현하기가 여간 어렵지 않다. 하지만 대개는 매우 소박한 자연이나 일상의 경험을 나타내는 것으로 시작된다. 그리고 되풀이해서 강물이라는 주제로 회귀하는 것을 보게 되는데, 이는 영속과 재생, 죄와 구원, 과거와 미래, 순간과 영원…… 등에 대한 생각을 가장 잘 포착하는 주제이기도 하다.

구상의 여러 시에는, 가령 「그리스도 폴의 강江」에서 보듯, 불교의 경향도 강하게 드러난다. 다른 많은 사람들과 마찬가지로 그도, 인간과 물질세계의 양면적인 관계, 시간과 영원 사이에 갇혀 있는 육체적 존재의 도전 등에 매료된다. 사실, 특히 그를 매료시킨 영어단어 가운데 하나는 '형이상학'이라는 낱말이다. 그의 작품에는 '신'神이라는 말이 거의 나오지 않지만, 그의 작품들 깊은 곳에는 신이 현존하고 있다.

많은 경우 구상은 가볍고 명랑한 어조를 채택하며 그 속에 깊은 의미를 결합시키는데, 이런 식으로 그는 현대의 많은 오염된 강물을 오염된 인간 내면의 이미지로 이용한다. 하지만 여기서도 그는 강물이 순수한 광대무변의 바다로 흘러들 듯 희망을 발견한다. 그리고 바로 이러한 미래 복원의 비전, 구상 부활의 희망 속에서 동양과 기독교 사상의 갈래들이 가장 놀랍게 통합되는 것이다.

고통에 대한 구상의 반응을 가장 잘 나타내는 낱말은 분명 '연민'일 텐데, 이것은 다른 사람의 고통을 함께 하는 타인에 대한 배려의 감정이다. '예언적' 목소리와 때때로 잘못 연결되곤 하는 비난조의 설교가 그의 시에는 거의 없거나 아예 없다. 구상에게 있어서는, 기독교 정신 특히 나자렛 예수가 매일매일의 일상적 현실에 숨어 있는 신비를 푸는 열쇠로 작용한다.

이런 비전이 있기에 그는 하루하루 삶의 작은 일상적 사건들을 찬양할 수 있고, 사회적·정치적 불의로 가득 찬 구체적인 현실을 절망없이 마주할 수 있는 것이다. 이와 동일한 신비는 또한 비어 있음과 가득 차 있음을 동시에 아우르는 태허太虛라는 보다 동양적인 언어로 표현되기도 한다.

궁극적으로, 구상의 시에서 우리가 얻게 되는 인상은 자신의 살아 있음에 매료되며, 하루하루가 드러나는 모든 일에서 한없는 놀라움을 발견하며, 그것들이 또한 수많은 방법으로 표현될 수 있다는 것에 환호하는 사람의 그것이다. 때때로 구상은 동양과 서양의 대조와 대비를 표현하기 위해 로댕의 '생각하는 사람'의 이미지와 불상 가운데서 가장 아름다운 불상인 반가사유상, 지금은 교토에 있지만 한국에서 유래된 것이 분명한 이 목각불상을 나란히 세워 놓기도 한다. 그의 말대로, 이토록 비할 데 없이 경쾌한 접근의 가능성이 있는데, 그 누가 자진해서 골치아픈 문제들에 짓눌리기를 택하겠는가.

Introduction

Ku Sang was born in Seoul on 16 September, 1919 in a Korea which had been annexed by Japan some ten years before and was just beginning to express its deep desire for independence. From his earliest years, he was caught up in the dramatic events, and in the suffering, that are the stuff of modern Korean history. His life has mostly been spent in journalism and the world of public opinion, with periods in political prisons, and in university classrooms. Ku Sang has been a journalist, chief editorialist, foreign correspondent, an essayist, a dramatist, a teacher, and, above all, a poet. He has occupied such positions as the presidency of the Catholic Writers' Association, and of Korean P.E.N., and he has received many of the highest awards for his work. Ku Sang is one of the most esteemed literary figures in Korea, and he continues to find many readers.

In 1984, Ku Sang published a set of poems about his early years, 'Even the Knots on Quince Trees', and these poems describe his development through childhood and youth. In the first of them he recalls how, in the early 1920s, his family left Seoul and set off towards the Northern town of Wonsan which he still considers his true home. It will surprise no one familiar with Korean sensibility that the first remembered emotional experience was one of tears.

Ku Sang was born into a Catholic family and his elder brother was among the priests who disappeared into silence and presumed martyrdom in North Korea in 1950. Ku Sang attended minor seminary for a time, before 'running away'. Later he became a student at the University of Japan in Tokyo, exposed to all the radical currents of Western, particularly French, thought.

Through this time of crisis, in which he studied the philosophy of religions, it was in the end poetry which offered a way forward. Ku Sang returned from his studies a 'follower of isms' and in 1942 became a journalist in what is now North Korea. A few years later he found himself obliged to flee to the South, leaving members of his family in the North, including his mother.

Life in the South was not much more tender, and soon after the end of the Korean War(1950~53) he found himself in prison, having published his 'Democratic Accusations', essays against the corruptions of power. Ku Sang often mentions the cavities in his lungs, the result of the tuberculosis contracted in the course of these experiences.

In 1946, before escaping to the South, he published a first

collection of poems in Wonsan. The experience of the Korean War is recorded in the 'Wasteland Poems', first published in 1956. Here we find clearly the sense of national unity, the refusal to accept the division of Korea, which mark many of Ku Sang's poems. An important feature in these war poems is the rejection of all artifice. The poet offers simple evocations of scenes, or of nature, without complex poetic effects, and without too much explicit moralizing.

The theme of the world's impermanence has also become one of Ku Sang's main themes, in part by way of a pun, The 'Sang' of his name is the Chinese character meaning 'enduring', 'permanent', and in philosophical contexts it is part of the quest for the unchanging Real that is expressed, for example, in the opening lines of Lao Tzu. One group of Ku Sang's poems, particularly personal 'Impermanent I', is entitled in Korean *Ku-Sang-Mu-Sang*, the 'Mu' corresponding to the 'im' of 'impermanence'.

Ku Sang's poetry is frequently made rich in sense and allusion through his use of Chinese characters full of abstract, philosophical meanings that are often difficult for the present generation of young Koreans, and which cannot be represented by any equivalent in English translation. Yet the starting point is usually some very simple experience of nature, or of daily life. Time after time, the theme of the river returns, as the best focus for thoughts about continuity and renewal, sin and redemption, past and future, time and eternity. The influence of Buddhism is strong in many of Ku Sang's poems, for example, in 'Christopher's River'.

He is fascinated, like so many, by the ambivalence of the link between man and the material universe, by the challenge that physical existence, caught between time and eternity, represents. Indeed, one of the English words he feels particularly attracted by is the word 'metaphysical'. Although the word 'God' is almost never used, God is deeply present in his works. Much of the time Ku Sang adopts a light, amused tone, combined with deep meaning; thus he finds use even for the polluted aspect of many modern rivers as an image of the soiled inner man. Yet there too he finds hope, as the river flows into the purer immensities of the ocean. It is in his vision of a future restoration that the Oriental and the Christian strands most strikingly unite, in Ku Sang's Resurrection hope.

The word that best expresses Ku Sang's response to suffering must be 'compassion', that feeling for others which also involves suffering with them. There is little or nothing of the moralizing denunciations sometimes wrongly associated with the 'prophetic' voice. For Ku Sang, Christianity, in particular the person of Jesus of Nazareth, is the key to the hidden mystery within daily reality. It is that vision which allows him to celebrate the minute events of daily life, or confront the concrete realities of social and political wrongs without despair. That same mystery is also expressed in the more Oriental language of vast emptiness, the Void which is yet Fullness.

In the end, the impression we gain from Ku Sang's verse is that of a man intrigued to find himself alive, inexhaustibly surprised by all the things that each day reveals, delighted too by the many ways in which they can be expressed. Ku Sang sometimes expresses the confrontation and contrast between East and West by setting side by side the image of Man found in Rodin's 'Thinker' and the image found in that most beautiful of all ancient Buddhist sculptures, the Maitreya carved in wood now in Kyoto but so clearly Korean in origin. As he says, who would choose to be so overwhelmed with problems when there is the possibility of such incomparable lightness of approach?

차 례
Contents

머리말 *Introduction*

제1부
암비暗秘 *Dark Mystery*

나 · 22	23 · Myself
선정禪定 · 26	27 · Meditation
점경點景 · 30	31 · Here and There
조화造化 속에서 · 34	35 · Within Creation
겨울 과수원에서 · 38	39 · In a Winter Orchard
암비暗秘 · 42	43 · Dark Mystery
오도午禱 · 46	47 · Midday Prayer
한 알의 사과속에서 · 48	49 · Within an Apple
조약돌 · 50	51 · A Pebble
독락獨樂의 장章 · 52	53 · Concerning Secret Joys

제 2 부

구상무상具常無常 Impermanent I

만화漫畵 · 56	57 · Comic Dialogue
백련白蓮 · 58	59 · White Lotus
은행銀杏 · 60	61 · Gingko Trees
어느 정회情懷 · 62	63 · Certain
정경情景 · 66	67 · Touching Sights
고모역顧母驛 · 68	69 · Komo Station, Mother's Station
가을 병실病室 · 70	71 · An Autumn Sickroom
구상무상具常無常 · 76	77 · Impermanent I
부음訃音 · 78	79 · News of Death
임종예습臨終豫習 · 82	83 · Rehearsal for a Death-bed Scene
노경老境 · 84	85 · Old Age

제3부

드레퓌스의 벤취에서
From Dreyfus' Bench

수난受難의 장章 · 90   91 · On Suffering
출애굽기出埃及記 별장別章 · 94   95 · Addition to Exodus
수치羞恥 · 96   97 · Shame
드레퓌스의 벤취에서 · 98   99 · From Dreyfus' Bench
어느 까치들의 울음 · 102   103 · Weeping of Magpies
월남기행越南紀行 · 106   107 · Back from Vietnam
귀가歸家 · 114   115 · Homeward Journey
펜의 명銘 · 116   117 · The Pen

제4부
신령한 새싹 Spirit-filled Buds

무소부재無所不在 · 122	123 · In al Places
요한에게 · 130	131 · To John
그 분이 홀로서 가듯 · 134	135 · As He Walked Alone
성탄절聖誕節 고음苦吟 · 136	137 · Christmas Lament
부활송復活頌 · 138	139 · Easter Hymn
성모상 앞에서 · 142	143 · Before the Virgin's Statue
신령한 새싹 · 146	147 · Spirit-filled Buds
신령한 소유所有 · 148	149 · Spirit-filled Wealth
말씀의 실상實相 · 150	151 · The True Appearance of the Word
나자렛 예수 · 152	153 · Jesus of Nazareth

제5부
초생달 꽃밭 *Garden by Moonlight*

영춘무迎春舞 · 162　163 · Springtime Dances
봄 빨래 · 166　167 · Spring Washing
봄 국화 · 170　171 · Spring Chrysanthemums
하일서경夏日叙景 · 174　175 · Scenes of a Summer's Day
실향失鄕 바다 · 178　179 · Seaside in a Lost Homeland
달밤 · 182　183 · Moonlit Evening
초동初冬의 서정抒情 · 184　185 · Thoughts as Winter Comes
겨울 거리에서 · 188　189 · In a Winter Street

제6부
연작시 Poem Cycles

모과木瓜	Even the Knots
옹두리에도 사연이 · 194	195 · on Quince Trees
초토焦土의 시 · 220	221 · Wasteland Poems
밭 일기日記 · 230	231 · Diary of the Fields
그리스도 폴의 강江 · 248	249 · Christopher's River

구상연보 · 277

『한국문학 영역총서』를 펴내며 · 282

제1부

암비暗秘
Dark Mystery

나

내 안에 사지四肢를 버둥거리는
어린애들처럼
크고 작은 밤 희노애락喜怒哀樂의 뿌리
그보다도

미닫이에 밤 그림자같이
꼬리를 휘젓는 육근六根이나 칠죄七罪의
심해어深海魚보다도
옹기굴 속 무명無明을 지나
원죄原罪와 업보業報의 마당에
널려 있는 우주진宇宙塵보다도

또다시 거품으로 녹아 흐르고
마른 풀같이 바삭거리는
원초原初와 시간의 지층을 빠져 나가서
사막에 치솟는 샘물과
빙하氷河의 균열龜裂, 오오 입자粒子의 파열破裂!

그보다도
광막廣漠한 우주 안에
좁쌀알보다, 작게 떠 있는
지구보다도

Myself

It is more than
the deep roots of every emotion, big or small,
of every kind, that squirm and kick
like little children somewhere inside

and more than
the deep - sea fish of six senses and seven sins,
that waves its tail
like a night - time shadow on a window pane
more, too, than
star - dust littering the yards
of Original Sin and Karma,
passing through the darkness of the potter's kiln

and more than
the oasis spring gushing from the desert sand,
melting again into foam and flowing
after filtering through strata of origins and time
with their rustle of dry grass,
and the crack in the glacier, or even exploding particles

more, too, than
the world, itself smaller
than a millet seed in the cosmic vastnesses

억조광년億兆光年의 별빛을 넘은
허막虛漠의 바다에
충만해 있는 에테르보다도

그 충만이 주는 구유具有보다도
그 반대의 허무虛無보다도
미지未知의 죽음보다도

보다 더 큰
우주 안의 소리 없는 절규!
영원을 안으로 품은 방대尨大!

나.

and more than
the ether — fullness of the boundless void
reaching beyond billions of light years of starlight

more, too, than
the substantiality such fullness gives,
and more than its opposing nihility,
more, too, than unknown death

more, greater,
a soundless cosmic shout!
An immensity embracing Eternity!

Myself.

선정禪定

늙은 바위 번들번들한 뒷머리에
푸른 벌레가 알을 슬듯
파릇파릇 이끼가 돋아 있다.

백곡百穀이 움트는 봄비의 소치所致런가?
아니면 백세百歲 바위의
소생하는 유치幼稚런가?

이제 꽃도 열매도
잎사귀도 소용치 않고
비바람도 천둥 번개도 들리지 않고
밤도 낮도 분간이 없고
악취나 향내도 모르고
과거와 현실과 꿈이 다를 바 없는
경계境界.

바위의 안은 암거暗渠의 흐름이 아니라
아침의 햇살을 받은 영창映窓의 청명淸明!
하늘의 저 허허창창虛虛蒼蒼과도 면오面晤하고

이 지상地上, 버라이어티의 문란紊亂도 관용寬容하고
저 대양大洋의 넘실거림도
홀로의 묵좌默坐로서 진정鎭靜한다.

Meditation

On the gleaming flank of an age-old rock,
lying like the eggs of some green insect,
fresh green moss is growing.

Is it an effect of the spring rain
that germinates the grain? Or a return
of infancy in this centuries-old stone?

Here and now is an inevitable condition
where flowers, fruit, and leaves too,
are useless, neither winds and rain,
nor thunder and lightning are heard,
without distinction of day and night,
and knowing nothing of stench and perfume,
no separation of past, and real, and dream.

Within the rock, no flow of filth, but
the brightness of a window in the morning sunlight!
In its communion with heaven's vastness,

accepting all the chaos of this world's variety-show,
by simply sitting there in silent meditation
it stills the ocean's tumult.

"그러나 나는 알라딘의 램프가 아니다!"

무심無心한 바위에
세심細心히 낀 이끼
선정禪定의 광경이여!

"But I am no Aladdin's lamp!"

Ah, moss so prudently clinging
to the indifferent rock!
True image of Meditation!

점경點景

산허리 무밭가
춘곤春困에 조는 늙은 바위에
쉬파리 한 마리 놀고 있다.

영嶺으로 오르는 산길 풀섶에
묵은 남비뚜껑만한 쇠똥엘
뻔질나게 드나들면서
바위의 응달진 허리에도 붙어 보고
햇볕에 단 이마에도 앉아 보고
움푹 파인 숫구멍에 괸
빗물에 촉촉히 젖어도 보고

손발을 살살 빌어도 보고
눈곱 같은 찌를 깔겨도 보고
서캐 같은 알을 슬어도 보고

이번엔 무밭 한가운데 홍일점紅一點끼어든
봄 국화 꽃술에 날아가 앉아서
영사막映寫幕에 홀린 소년처럼
지평선까지 평면으로 전개된
들과 강과 길을 내려다보는데

Here and There

A turnip field on a mountainside.
Around an ancient, springtime-drowsy rock
a single blowfly buzzes.

It comes and goes, all the time,
among old, panlid-like pats of dung
that lie in the grass on the crestward path,
now perching low on the rock's shaded waist,
now squatting high on its sunburned brow,
now moistening itself at the stagnant water
held in deep pits on its rocky crown,

then delicately folding its legs in prayer,
depositing spots of pustular waste
or laying tiny, nit-like eggs,

then flying off to a spring chrysanthemum's stamens,
a single red spot in the midst of the turnip field,
and there, like a boy hypnotized by a cinema screen,
staring down at fields, rivers, roads,
as they stretch out level to the far horizon

세상은 일시에 모두 정지되어
푸른 송장이 된 것같이
숨소리도 없는 이 순간,
기아飢餓와 멸시蔑視와 살육殺戮에서 해방된 순간
저주詛呪와 모반謀反도 없는 이 순간,

너, 쉬파리 똥파리
어쩐지 이 고요가
서러운 공포가 되며
산울림하게 왕왕, 울어 보누나.

and suddenly the world seems all suspended,
like a green, dead body,
a moment without the sound of breathing,
a moment free of starvation, disdain, slaughter,
this moment, without curses or conspiring,

and somehow, blowfly, dungfly,
as if for you this stillness
bred a grieving fear,
echoing, your buzzing seems to weep.

조화造化 속에서

울밑 장독대를 빙 둘러
채송화가 피어 있다.

희고 연연한 몸매에
색색의 꽃술을 달고
저마다 간드러진 태를 짓고
서로 어깨를 떠밀기도 하고
얼굴을 비비기도 하며 피어 있다.

하늘엔 수박달이 높이 걸리고
이슬이 젖어드는 이슥한 밤인데
막내딸 가슴의 브로우치만큼씩한
죄그만 나비들이 찾아 들어
꽃술 위를 하늘하늘 날고 있다.

노랑,
빨강,
분홍,
연두,
보라,
자주,

Within Creation

Beneath the fence, round the storage platform,
the rose moss blooms.

With multi-colored stamens
crowning the soft white stems
they flirt there, posing,
nudging and jostling,
rubbing their cheeks, they bloom.

A water-melon moon perches high in the sky;
the night, nearly spent, is moist with dew,
and tiny butterflies no larger than the brooch
on my younger daughter's breast,
come hovering lightly over the stamens,

yellow,
red,
pink,
green,
violet,
purple,

이 꽃술에서 저 꽃술로
꽃가루를 옮겨 나르는 나비들!
이른 봄부터 밤마저 새워가며
그 수도 없이 날던 나비 떼들!

알록달록 채송화의 꽃물을 들이기에
저 미물微物들이 여러 천 년을 거듭하는
억만億萬의 역사役事를 하였겠구나.

헛간 뒤 감나무의 짓무른 홍시도
입추立秋 전까지는 입이 부르트게 떫었으며
저 뒷동산의 밤송이도
가시를 곤두세워 얼씬도 못하게 하더니만
알을 익혀 하강下降의 기름칠을 하고는
입을 제 스스로 벌렸다.

오오, 만물은 저마다
현신現身과 내일의 의미를 알고
서로가 서로를 지성至誠으로 도와
저렇듯 어울리며 사는데

사람인 나 홀로 이 밤
울타리에 썩어 가는 말뚝이듯
아무것도 모르며 섰는가?

these butterflies, flitting from stamen to stamen
in pollen quest!
Swarms of butterflies, since spring began,
even by night, flying innumerable!

Thus bringing colors to the rainbow flowers
over thousands of years, how huge a task
these tiny things have performed, to be sure!

Behind the shed soft persimmons hang red;
before, they would shrivel your mouth;
on the hill above, the chestnuts
bristled with spines to keep strangers at bay;
but now the nuts are ripe and shine ready to fall,
they open their mouths of their own accord.

Ah, every creature, every one,
knows the meaning of here, and tomorrow,
and so they live in togetherness,
assisting each other with all their hearts;

so how is it that I, a man, stand here
this night, all alone, like a rotting stick in a fence,
understanding nothing?

겨울 과수원에서

흰 눈이 소금같이 뿌려진
과수원에

한 그루 매화의 굵고 검은 가지가
승리의 V자를 지었고
그 언저리를 부활의 화관花冠인 듯
꽃이 만발하다.

"보라! 나의 안에 생명을 둔 자
죽어도 죽지 않으리니
보이지 않는 실재實在를
너희는 의심치 말라."

까치가 한 마리 이 가지 저 가지를
해롱대며 날은다.

폐肺의 공동空洞처럼 뻥 뚫린 구덩이 옆에
한 그루 아름드리 사과나무가
송장처럼 뻐드러져 있다.

그림자처럼 어두운 사내가
지게를 지고 와서
도끼로 마른 가지를 쳐내고
몸뚱이를 패서 지고 간다.

In a Winter Orchard

In the orchard white with snow
like sprinkled salt,
a plum tree raises thick black branches
in a victory sign,
outlined with flowers in full bloom,
like an Easter garland.

"Behold, whoever puts his life in me,
even though he dies, will never die;
do not be doubtful
of invisible realities."

Playfully, a single magpie
hops from branch to branch.

By a hole gaping like a cavity in a lung,
stiff as a corpse
an apple tree lies, a full arm's girth.

A man comes by, dark as shade,
with a frame bound upon his back;
he lops the dead branches with an axe,
splits the trunk, and bears it all away.

"보라! 형벌의 불아궁 속으로 던져질
망자亡者의 몰골을,
그러므로 너희는 현존現存의 뿌리를
병들지 않도록 삼가라."

얼어붙은 하늘에 까마귀가
까옥까옥 날은다.

"Behold, a figure of the dead
who will tomorrow be cast
into perdition's flames; beware, then,
lest the roots of your existence become infected!"

A crow flies cawing
across the frozen sky.

암비 暗秘

그 감방監房에 깔린 양탄자에는
꽉 차리만큼 큰 무늬의
황금해바라기가 불타고 있다.

팔각八角의 창에는
도시의 대양大洋이 넘실거리며
공장工場 군함軍艦과 아파트 기선汽船과
자질구레한 판잣집 쪽배가 떠 있다.

하늘에는 이 시가를 휘덮는
검고 큰 박쥐가 새끼 박쥐를 거느리고
줄에 매여 날고 있고
방 속엔 발가벗은 사내가 무릎을 꿇고서
엄지와 검지로
노랑나비를 붙잡아 먹으려고
입을 크게 벌리고 있다.

제물로 짜진 한 벽 거울엔
그의 그림자 같은 제3의 사내가
입을 벌리고 춤을 추며
또 다른 나비를 쫓고 있고
맞은 벽은 예리한 칼날이 꽂힌 철창이
한 떨기 꽃이 핀 절벽과 마주하고 있다.

Dark Mystery

On the carpet spread in the prison cell,
so large that it fills the whole design,
a golden sunflower blazes.

Beyond the octagonal window
the city surges like ocean waves,
with factory-warships and high-rise steamers,
to say nothing of the slum shack cockle-boats.

In the sky, hovering over the city
as if attached to a cord,
a great black bat flies, leading her young,
while in the room a naked man,
kneeling, opens wide his mouth,
about to devour a yellow butterfly
caught between his finger and thumb.

In the looking-glass built into one wall
a third man, like the other's reflection, dances
open-mouthed in pursuit of another butterfly
while in the opposite wall a barred window,
edged with sharp knives, looks onto a sheer cliff
where a single flower is blooming.

나의 심상心象은 암비暗秘 속에서
구원도 없는 광명을 향해
아름답게 울고 있다.

Within this Mystery, my image
is beautifully weeping
towards a light that offers no salvation.

오도午禱

저 허공虛空과 나 사이 무명無明의 장막을 거두어 주오.
이 땅 위의 모든 경계선境界線과 철망과 담장을
거두어 주오.
사람들의 미움과 탐욕과 차별지差別智*를 거두어 주오.
나와 저들의 체념과 절망을 거두어 주오.

소생케 해 주오. 나에게 놀람과 눈물과 기도를,
소생케 해 주오. 죽은 모든 이들의 꿈과 사랑을,
소생케 해 주오. 인공이 빚어낸 자연의 모든 파상破傷을.

그리고 허락하오. 저 바위에게 말을, 이 바람에게 모습을,
오오, 나에게 순수의 발광체發光體로 영생永生할 것을
허락하오.

---

* 차별지差別智 ; 만물 만상의 근본을 평등하게 보지 않고 차등 현상으로 보는
인식.

Midday Prayer

Take away this darkling veil
    that lies between myself and space.
Take away from off the earth all boundary lines,
    all fences and all walls.
Take away all human hatred,
    greed, and all discrimination.
Take away surrender and despair,
    both mine and theirs.

Restore to me wonder, tears and prayer.
Restore the dreams and loves of all the dead.
Restore the hurts that humans inflict on Nature.

And grant words to that rock, a face to this breeze,
and oh, to me grant to live eternally
as a radiancy of purity.

한 알의 사과 속에는

한 알의 사과 속에는
구름이 논다.

한 알의 사과 속에는
대지大地가 숨쉰다.

한 알의 사과 속에는
강이 흐른다.

한 알의 사과 속에는
태양이 불탄다.

한 알의 사과 속에는
달과 별이 속삭인다.

그리고 한 알의 사과 속에는
우리의 땀과 사랑이 영생永生한다.

Within an Apple

Within a single apple's sphere
the clouds drift by.

Within a single apple's sphere
the good earth breathes.

Within a single apple's sphere
the river flows along.

Within a single apple's sphere
the sun blazes down.

Within a single apple's sphere
moon and stars whisper.

And within a single apple's sphere
our striving and our loving live eternal.

조약돌

집 앞 행길에서
그 어느 날 발부리에 채운
조약돌 하나와 나날이 만난다.

처음에 우리는 그저 심드렁하게
아침 저녁 서로 스쳐 지냈지만
돌은 차츰 나에게 말도 걸어오고
슬그머니 손도 내밀어
친구처럼 익숙해갔다.

그리고 아침이면 돌은
안으로부터 은총의 꽃을 피워
나를 축복해 주고
늦은 밤에도 졸지 않고
나의 안녕安寧을 기다려 준다.

때로는 천사처럼 훌훌 날아서
내 방엘 찾아 들어와
만남의 신비를 타이르기도 하고
사귐의 불멸을 일깨워도 준다.

나는 이제 그 돌을 만날 때마다
미개未開하고 불안스런 나의 현존現存이
부끄러울 뿐이다.

A Pebble

On the path before my house
every day I meet a pebble
that once was kicked by my passing toe.

At first we just casually
brushed past each other, morning and night,
but gradually the stone began to address me
and furtively reach out a hand,
so that we grew close, like friends.

And now each morning the stone,
blooming inwardly with flowers of Grace,
gives me its blessing,
and even late at night
it waits watchfully to greet me.

Sometimes, flying as on angels' wings
it visits me in my room
and explains to me the Mystery of Meeting,
reveals the immortal nature of Relationship.

So now, whenever I meet the stone,
I am so uncivilized and insecure
that I can only feel ashamed.

독락獨樂의 장章

애들아, 내가 노니는 여기를
매화 옛 등걸에
까치집이라 하자.

늬들은 나를 환희幻戱에 산다고
기껏 웃어 주지만
나에게는 어느 영웅보다도
에누리 없는 사연이 있다.

이제 나도 세월도
서로 무심해지고
눈 아래 일렁이는 세파世波도
생사生死의 소음騷音도
설월雪月 같은 은은殷殷 속에
화해和解된 유정有情!

애들아!
박명薄明, 저 가지에 걸치는 요광饒光과
모혼暮昏의 정숙靜淑을 생식生食하면서
운명을 정서情緖로 응감應感시킨
내사 갖는 이 즐거움이야
늬들은 모르지.
도도陶陶한 이 아픔을
늬들은 모르지.

Concerning Secret Joys

Children! Let us imagine this place
where I am strolling, to be a magpie's nest
up in the branches of an old plum tree!

Ah! You reckon I am living in a fool's paradise
and it makes you laugh out loud;
yet I have things to tell, no exaggeration,
more than any hero has.

Nowadays, Time and I
have grown indifferent;
the wave-tossed world before my eyes,
this charivari of living and dying,
is reduced to a distant reverberation like
snow by moonlight, human sympathies reconciled.

Children! As I feast fresh, at break of day,
upon dawn's splendor spread along the branches
or upon the stillness of an evening twilight,
you simply cannot know
such joy as I experience then:
Fate made to correspond with feeling.
You simply cannot know
such happy pain.

제2부

구상무상具常無常
Impermanent I

만화漫畵

여보!
당신 몰루?
내가 찾는 것
그것 몰루?

당신마저 몰루?
이제는 찾는 내가
그것이 무엇인지 모르게 된
바로 그것 말이요.

내 속은 눈 감고도
환하다는 당신이
내가 한평생 찾고 있는
그것이 무엇인지
그것만은 몰루?
여보!

Comic Dialogue

Darling!
Don't you know?
The thing I'm looking for,
you don't know?

Don't even you know?
The thing I'm looking for now,
that thing, I don't know what it is,
that's the thing I mean!

And you say you can read my thoughts
even with your eyes closed!
That thing I've been looking for all my life,
what is it?
Don't you know?
Darling!

백련白蓮

내 가슴 무너진 터전에
쥐도 새도 모르게 솟아난 백련白蓮 한 떨기

사막인 듯 메마른 나의 마음에다
어쩌자고 꽃망울은 맺어 놓고야
이제 더 피울래야 피울 길 없는
백련白蓮 한 송이

온밤 내 꼬박 새워 지켜도
너를 가리울 담장은 없고
선머슴들이 너를 꺾어간다손
나는 냉가슴 앓는 벙어리될 뿐

오가는 길손들이 너를 탐내
송두리째 떠간다 한들
막을래야 막을 길 없는
내 마음에 망울진 백련白蓮 한 송이

차라리 솟지나 않았던들
세상 없는 꽃에도 무심할 것을
너를 가깝게 멀리 바라볼 때마다
퉁퉁 부어오르는 영혼의 눈시울.

White Lotus

In the wastelands of my heart, sprung up
unknown to mouse or bird, one white lotus.

In my desert-thirsty heart,
alas, why has this bud sprung up?
For now it should bloom,
but it finds no way,
this white lotus flower.

Although I anxiously watch all night,
you have no wall to shield you from harm:
suppose the urchins pluck you away?
I could only suffer, frozen, dumb.

Passers-by, coveting you,
may carry you off, root and all;
I ought to prevent that, but have no means,
bud in my heart of a white lotus flower.

If you had simply never sprung up at all,
I would not have cared, most special flower;
but now, when I see you near by or afar,
the lids of the eyes of my soul inflame.

은행銀杏
—우리 부부의 노래

나 여기 서 있노라.
나를 바라고 틀림없이
거기 서 있는
너를 우러러
나 또한 여기 서 있노라.

이제사 달가운 꿈자리커녕
입맞춤도 간지러움도 모르는
이렇듯 넉넉한 사랑의 터전 속에다
크낙한 순명順命의 뿌리를 박고서
나 너와 마주 서 있노라.

일월日月은 우리의 연륜年輪을 묶혀 가고
철따라 잎새마다 꿈을 익혔다
뿌리건만

오직 너와 나와의
열매를 맺고서
종신終身토록 이렇게
마주 서 있노라.

Gingko Trees

—A Song of our Marriage

Here I stand.
Turned towards you
who steadfastly wait for me,
standing there;
so too I stand here.

Now is quite unlike sweet dreamland,
no response to kisses and tickling, at all;
but as we have put down deep roots of submission
into the ground of this generous loving,
you and I stand face to face.

Days, months pass, leave in us rings of the years;
with the seasons, dreams ripen between every leaf,
then scatter,

while we simply bear fruit,
yours and mine,
as we stand for a lifetime
face to face.

어느 정회情懷

한차례 공동묵상共同默想을 마친 후
성모상이 서 있는
수도원 숲 그늘에
뿔뿔이 쉬는 참이었다.

곱살히 늙어 가는 여교우女敎友 한 분이
내 옆 통나무 의자에 다가와 앉더니
"송도원松濤園* 앞동네가 바로 저의 고향이거든요.
40년 전 마당 앞 행길을 지나가시던 선생님을 뵙고는
그만 넋을 잃고서 평생을 잊을 수가 없었어요.
착실하고 무던한 남편을 만나 별로 고생도
모르고 살아오고
아들 딸 여럿 낳고 손주도 보았는데
선생님의 모습이 끝내 지워지지가 않는군요.
신문 잡지에서 선생님 함자銜字나 사진을 뵈면
가슴이 두근거리면서 반가왔고요.
선생님 쓰신 글은 찾아가면서 죄 읽었지요.
어쩌면 제가 성당엘 다니게 된 것도
선생님을 따라서예요.
선생님은 이런 푸념 같은 얘기
들으시기 매우 거북하실 줄 아오나
제 생전 한 번만은 만나 뵙고 털어놓고 싶었어요."
하고선 맑은 아미蛾眉를 숙였다.

Certain Touching Memories

After one group meditation session
we had a break for relaxation
in the shade of the convent grove
where a statue of the Virgin stood.

A delicately aging lady of the parish
came and sat beside me on a log bench ; she began :
"The region near Songdowon*, that is where I am from!
Forty years ago, the mere sight of you
passing down the road in front of our yard
was enough to make me lose my senses,
and the memory has lasted a whole lifetime.
Oh, I met a nice reliable husband,
have encountered no great problems in life,
I have had several children and now
I have grandchildren too, but your image has never faded.
Whenever I saw your name or your picture in the press
my heart would always beat faster for joy.
I have got and read all you have ever written.
And if I now go to church, that too is by your example.
Of course, I know it must be embarrassing for you
to hear this kind of crazy talk ;
but I did so want, just once in my life,
to meet you and tell you all these things!"
she said, and gracefully lowered her eyes.

나는 응답할 말이 없는지라
"진작 좀 말씀을 하시지 그랬어요?"
기롱譏弄으로 받았더니 그녀도
"선생님이 이렇듯 수월하게 받아 주실 줄 미처
알았어야죠?"
개운하게 응수를 해와서
서로 쳐다보고 활짝 웃었다.

이때 울려 퍼지는 집합 벨소리
우리는 함께 늙은 부부처럼
나란히 기도소祈禱所로 향했다.

* 송도원松濤園; 내 고향 원산元山에 있는 유명한 해수욕장.

I could find no reply;
"Perhaps, if you had only said this before……"
I joked.

"I could scarcely anticipate how lightly
you would take it", she promptly retorted, to my relief.
We looked at each other, and beamed broadly.

At that moment came the sound of the assembly bell,
so side by side, like an elderly couple,
we duly made our way to the chapel.

* *Songdowon ; a famous beach near the poet's childhood home in Wonsan.*

정경情景

가을의 창백한 오후 해가 드리운
피아노 건반鍵盤 뚜껑 위
스타킹 한 켤레가 얹혀 있다.

외국外國서 사는 딸애가
아침에 떠나면서
떨구고 간 것이리라.

나는 이 정물靜物이 서투르면서도
몹시 낯익어
기억을 더듬고 더듬은 끝에

대구大邱 약전藥廛골 뒷골목
어느 기방妓房에서 눈을 뜬 아침
머리맡 문갑文匣 위에 놓여 있던
버선 두 짝을 떠올렸다.

이와 함께 오일도吳一島의 시詩,
"빈 가지에 바구니 걸어 놓고
내 소녀는 어디로 갔느뇨"라는
구절句節을 중얼거렸다.

Touching Sights

Touched by an autumn afternoon's pale sunlight,
on the piano keyboard lid
lies a pair of stockings.

They must have been laid aside
by my daughter who is living abroad
when she was leaving this morning.

Seeing this still-life composition, so strange
yet so completely familiar,
after fumbling and groping in my memories:

In Taegu, down a narrow lane behind the herb market,
opening my eyes in a singing-girl's room one morning
and, laid on a chest beside my pillow,
two stocking slippers come to mind.

At the same moment I begin to murmur
a phrase from a poem by O Il-Do:
"On a tree's bare branch her basket hangs,
where then has my darling gone?"

고모역顧母驛

고모역顧母驛을 지나칠 양이면
어머니가 기다리신다.
대문 밖에 나오셔 기다리신다.
이제는 아내보다도 별로 안 늙으신
그제 그 모습으로
38선 넘던 그 날 바래 주시듯
행길까지 나오셔 기다리신다.

천방지축 하루 해를 보내고
책가방에 빈 도시락을 쩔렁대며
통학차通學車로 돌아오던 어릴 때처럼
이제는 아버지가 돌아가실 때만큼이나
머리가 희어진 나를
역까지 나오셔 기다리신다.

이북 고향에 홀로 남으신 채
그 생사조차 모르는 어머니가
예까지 오셔서 기다리신다.

Komo Station, Mother's Station

Whenever I pass Komo* Station,
my mother is waiting.
Out in front of the garden gate, she is waiting,
looking scarcely older than my wife looks now,
looking just as when she saw me off
the day I crossed the 38th Parallel,
out in the lane, she is waiting.

Living helter-skelter, day by day,
rattling the empty lunch-box in my satchel,
coming home from school by train, as in that childhood,
so now when my hair is as grey
as my father's was when he died,
out by the station she is waiting.

My mother, who stayed behind
alone in our North Korean home,
alive still, or dead, I do not know,
has come here now and is waiting.

* *Komo is on the outskirts of Taegu, South Korea, and its name means "Mother-caring".*

가을 병실病室

가을 하늘에
기러기 떼 날아간다.
내 앓는 가슴 위에다
긴 그림자를 지으며
북으로 날아간다.
한 마리 한 마리 꼬리를 물듯이
일직선一直線을 그으며 날아간다.

팔락
    팔락
        팔락
            팔락
                팔락
                    팔락
                        팔락
내 가슴 공동空洞에 내려 앉는다.
                    도
                레
              미
            파
          솔
        라
시

An Autumn Sickroom

In the autumn sky
flocks of wild geese fly away.
Casting long shadows
over my aching heart,
northwards they fly.
Each seems to hold the other's tail
as in straight lines they fly away.

Flapping
      flapping
           flapping
                 flapping
                      flapping
                            flapping
                                  flapping
                                       flapping
they drop down and settle in the cavities in my breast.
                                                  do
                                          re
                                mi
                       fa
              sol
        la
ti

마지막 한 마리는
내가 붙잡았다.

     팔딱
     팔딱
     팔딱
내 가슴이 뛴다.
     끼럭
     끼럭
     끼럭
내 가슴이 운다.

끼럭
끼럭
끼럭
하늘이 운다.
     끼럭
끼럭
나는 놓아 보낸다.

혼자 떨어져 날으는 뒷모습이
나 같다.

the last one
I captured.

>throb
>throb
>throb

my heart is racing.
>honk
>honk
>honk

my heart is weeping.

honk
honk
honk
the sky is weeping.
>honk

honk
I set it free.

That single, lonely, flying form
is like me.

가을 하늘에
기러기 떼 날아간다.
나의 가슴에
평행선平行線을 그으며 날아간다.

In the autumn sky
flocks of wild geese fly away,
within my heart
in parallel lines they fly away.

구상무상 具常無常

이제 세월처럼 흘러가는
남의 세상 속에서
가쁘던 숨결은 식어가고
뉘우침마저 희미해 가는 가슴.

나보다도 진해진 그림자를
밟고 서면
꿈결 속에 흔들리는 갈대와 같이
그저 심심해 서 있으면
해어진 호주머니 구멍으로부터
바람과 추억이 새어나가고
꽁초도 사랑도 흘러 나가고
무엇도 무엇도 떨어져 버리면

나를 취케 할 아편도 술도 없어
홀로 깨어 있노라.
아무렇지도 않노라.

Impermanent I

Nowadays, in that world of other people
that flows away like Time,
my formerly panting breath subsides,
and even repentance grows faint in my breast.

As I tread on my shadow,
now more real than myself,
and stand aimlessly
like a reed waving in a dream,
and from a hole in my worn pocket
hopes and memories leak away,
fag ends and loves drop away,
bit by bit everything falls away,

no drug or drink to drown things in,
alone, awake, I stand.
Nothing matters at all.

부음訃音

이 봄엔
친구의 부음訃音이
사흘도리다.

아까운 이가 먼저 간다.

시인詩人의 수입으론
영결永訣도 거른다.

영전靈前에 설 때마다
다음은 내 차례지 싶다.

아무런 준비가 없다.

삶도 부실했거니와
가족이나 세상에게
너무나 잘못했다.

저승 가서도 부모님이랑
이웃이랑 뵐 낯이 없다.

더구나 하느님께는
두렵기만 하다.

News of Death

This spring
news of a friend's death
came twice within three days.

The ones we love and miss go first.

A poet's income being what it is,
I avoid funerals.

Whenever I stand before someone dead
I feel it's my turn next.

But nothing at all is ready.

My life has been far too unfaithful,
I have failed my family
and the world too much.

And when I enter the other world,
I shall be ashamed to meet parents or neighbors.

And then, towards God
I feel nothing but dread.

허지만 나의 부음訃音도
어차피 멀지 않다.

Yet news of my death
cannot be long in coming.

임종예습臨終豫習

흰 홑이불에 덮여
앰뷸런스에 실려간다.

밤하늘이 거꾸로 발 밑에 드리우며
죽음의 아슬한 수렁을 짓는다.

이 채로 굳어 뻗어진 내 송장과
사그라져 앙상한 내 해골이 떠오른다.

돌이켜보아야 착오 투성이 한평생
영원의 동산에다 꽃 피울 사랑커녕
땀과 눈물의 새싹도 못 지녔다.

이제 허둥댔자 부질없는 노릇이지……

"아버지 저의 영혼을
당신 손에 맡기나이다"

시늉만 했지 옳게 섬기지는 못한
그 분의 최후 말씀을 부지중不知中 외우면서
나는 모든 상념想念에서 벗어난다.

또 숨이 차온다.

Rehearsal for a Death-bed Scene

Lying under a white sheet,
I am carried off in an ambulance.

The evening sky hangs upside-down beneath my feet,
forming a terrible quagmire of death.

I picture my corpse like this, rigid, stretched out,
my skeleton, decomposed, reduced to bones.

Behind me, a lifetime lies smothered in error,
I have not even born buds of sweat and tears,
let alone the love that can blossom in Eternity.

No point in getting flustered now……

"Father, into your hands
I commend my spirit."

Instinctively repeating the last words of Him
whom I have only aped, not truly served,
I sever the link with all concepts.

And my breath becomes rasping.

노경 老境

여기는 결코 버려진 땅이 아니다.

영원의 동산에다 꽃 피울
신령한 새싹을 가꾸는 새 밭이다.

젊어서는 보다 육신을 부려왔지만
이제는 보다 정신의 힘을 써야 하고
아울러 잠자던 영혼을 일깨워
형이상形而上의 것에 눈을 떠야 한다.

무엇보다 고독의 망령亡靈에 사로잡히거나
근심과 걱정을 도락道樂으로 알지 말자.

고독과 불안은 새로운 차원의
탄생을 재촉하는 은혜이어니
육신의 노쇠와 기력의 부족을
도리어 정신의 기폭제起爆劑로 삼아
삶의 진정한 쇄신에 나아가자.

관능적官能的 즐거움이 줄어들수록
인생과 자신의 모습은 또렷해지느니
믿음과 소망과 사랑을 더욱 불태워
저 영원의 소리에 귀 기울이자.

Old Age

Here we are in no abandoned waste.

It is rather a fresh field, nurturing mysterious buds
that will only blossom in Eternity's land.

In youth we tended to wield our bodies
but now we must use strength of mind,
and as we rouse up our sleepy souls
we must apply our attention to metaphysical things.

Above all, let us not be slaves to specters of loneliness,
not experience cares and concerns as distractions.

Loneliness and insecurity are graces
announcing the birth of a new dimension;
using now the body's aging, and the lack of energy,
as stimuli offered to the mind,
let us advance towards life's true renewal.

The less the joys of the flesh become,
the clearer we see both life and self;
so, as the flames of faith, hope, and love burn brighter,
let us listen more closely to Eternity's voice.

이제 초목草木의 잎새나 꽃처럼
계절마다 피고 스러지던
무상無常한 꿈에서 깨어나

죽음을 넘어 피안彼岸에다 피울
찬란하고도 불멸不滅하는 꿈을 껴안고
백금白金같이 빛나는 노년老年을 살자.

Now let us awake from this illusory dream
where, like the leaves and blossoms of Nature,
all blooms and vanishes with the seasons,

and cherishing a glorious, undying dream
that will bloom beyond death, on another shore,
let us live an old age as radiant as silver.

제3부

드레퓌스의 벤취에서
From Dreyfus' Bench

수난受難의 장章

우 몰려 온다. 돌팔매가 날아온다.
머슴애들은 수수깡에 쇠똥을 꿰매달고
어른들은 곡괭이를 휘저으며 마구 쫓아오는데
돌아서서 눈물을 찔끔 흘리고
선지피가 쏟아지는 이마를 감싸 쥐고서
어머니 얼굴도 떠오르지 않는데
나는 이제 어디메로 달려야 하는가.

쫓기다가 쫓기다가 숨었다.
상여집으로 숨었다.
애비 욕, 에미 망신 고래고래 터뜨리며
벌 떼처럼 에워싸고 빙빙 돌아가는데
나는 얼른 상여 뚜껑을 열어 제치고
벌떡 드러누워 숨을 꼭 죽였다.

피를 토한 듯 후련해지는 가슴이여
술 취한 듯 홍그러워지는 마음이여
사람도 도깨비도 얼씬 못하는 상여 속에서
나는 어느 새 달디단 꿈 한 자리를 엮고 있었다.

상여 속에 송장처럼 잠들은
사나이 얼굴은 십상 달같이 흴 게다.
어쩌면 상달같이 깜찍한 여인이
별 같은 두 눈을 반짝이며

On Suffering

They come storming on. Stones fly.
The boys wield dung-bound millet stalks,
older men swing hoes as they come in rough pursuit,
I turn and stand, tears trickling down,
sheltering a brow from which blood thickly oozes,
no sign of mother's face here,
where can I run to now?

Pursued and again pursued, I hid.
In the hut where they keep the hearse, I hid.
Insults, deep disgrace, shouts of anger,
round and round like a swarm of bees they turned
while I quickly pushed open the lid of the hearse,
jumped in, lay down, and held my breath.

My breast grew cool, like after coughing blood,
my heart grew light, like after drinking wine;
in the hearse, that no man or ghost dares approach,
I found myself weaving a scene from a sweet dream.

The face of one resting like a corpse in a hearse,
must seem white as the full moon itself.
A girl, sly as the harvest moon,
eyes twinkling stars,

내 상처에 향기로운 기름을 바르고 있을 풍경
나의 달가운 꿈 속의 꿈이여.

추억의 연못가엔 사랑의 연꽃도 한 송이 피었으리.
다홍신은 벗어 놓고 외로움에
장승처럼 못박혀 있는
또 나의 사랑.

꽃수레처럼 화려한 상여를 타고
림보*로 향하는 길 위엔
곡성마저 즐겁구나
소복한 나의 여인아
사흘만 참으라.

* 림보; 예수가 죽어서 부활하기 전, 선령善靈이 먼저 머물던 곳. 일명 고성소
 古聖所.

seemed to be pouring sweet oil upon my wounds:
a dream within my sweet dream.

In by the pond of memory a lotus of love bloomed.
That other love was riven to loneliness,
she stood there alone, like a statue, a log,
having put off her scarlet shoes.

Riding the hearse, bright as a cartload of flowers,
and following the road towards Limbo,
even the noise of keening is joyful!
Ah, my darling in mourning white,
only wait for the third day to come.

출애굽기出埃及記 별장別章

각설却說, 이 때에 저들도
황금의 송아지를 만들어 섬겼다.

믿음이나 진실, 사랑과 같은
인간살이의 막중한 필수품들은
낡은 지팡이나 헌신짝처럼 버려지고
서로 다투어 사람의 탈만 쓴
짐승들이 되어갔다.

세상은 아론*의 무리들이 판을 치고
이에 노예근성이 꼬리를 쳤다.

그 속에도 시나이 산에서 내려올
모세를 믿고 기다리는 사람들이
외롭지만 있었다.

자유의 젖과 꿀이 흐르는
가나안!
후유, 멀고 험하기도 하다.

---

*아론; 구약성서 <출애굽기>에 나오는 인물로 황금 송아지 우상을 만드는
데 앞장섬.

Addition to Exodus

You know, in those days too they made
a golden calf and worshipped it.

Trust, sincerity or love,
such basic necessities of existence,
thrown aside like old sticks or worn-out boots,
they became beasts,
fighting one another, simply wearing human masks.

The world, with Aaron's hoardes in charge,
became a place of submissiveness.

But even then there were people
trusting, waiting for Moses to come down from Sinai,
simply, in solitude.

Ah, Canaan,
flowing with milk and honey!
Ah, far off and how hard to reach.

수치羞恥

창경원昌慶苑
철책鐵柵과 철망鐵網 속을 기웃거리며
부끄러움을 아는
동물을 찾고 있다.

여보, 원정園丁!
행여나 원숭이의
그 빨간 엉덩짝에
무슨 조짐이라도 없소?

혹시는 곰의 연신 핥는
발바닥에나
물개의 수염에나
아니면 잉꼬 암놈 부리에나
무슨 징후라도 없소?

이 도성都城 시민에게선
이미 퇴화된
부끄러움을
동물원에 와서 찾고 있다.

Shame

In the zoo,
peering between bars and netting,
I search for an animal
that knows what is shame.

I say, keeper!
Might there just possibly be
in those monkeys' red posteriors
at least some trace of it?

What of the bear's paw,
perpetually licked?
Or the seals' whiskers,
or maybe the parrot's beak?
Is there really no trace of it there?

Since shame
has vanished
from this city's people,
I came to the zoo to look for it.

드레퓌스의 벤취*에서

— 도형수徒刑囚 짱*의 독백獨白

빠삐용! 이제 밤바다는 설레는 어둠뿐이지만 코코 야자 자루에 실려 멀어져 간 자네 모습이야 내가 죽어 저승에 간들 어찌 잊혀질 건가!

빠삐용! 내가 자네와 함께 떠나지 않은 것은 그까짓 간수들에게 발각되어 치도곤治盜棍을 당한다거나, 상어나 돌고래들에게 먹혀 바다귀신이 된다거나, 아니면 아홉 번째인 자네의 탈주가 또 실패하여 함께 되옳혀 올 것을 겁내고 무서워해서가 결코 아닐세.

빠삐용! 내가 자네를 떠나보내기 전에 이 말만은 차마 못했네만 가령 우리가 함께 무사히 대륙에 닿아 자네가 그리 그리던 자유를 주고, 반가이 맞아 주는 복지福地가 있다 손, 나는 우리에게 새 삶이 없다는 것을 알게 되었단 말일세. 이 세상은 어디를 가나 감옥이고 모든 인간은 너나 없이 도형수徒刑囚임을 나는 깨달았단 말일세.

이 <죽음의 섬>을 지키는 간수의 사나운 눈초리를 받으며 우리 큰 감방의 형편없이 위험한 건달패들과 어울리면서 나의 소임인 200마리의 돼지를 기르고 사는 것이 딴 세상 생활보다 좋지도 나쁘지도 않다는 것을 터득했단 말일세.

From Dreyfus' Bench

— *Convict Jean's Soliloquy*

Papillon! Now the evening sea is nothing but a rocking darkness, but how could I ever forget the image of you drifting away on a coconut trunk, even though I die and pass to the other world!

Papillon! If I did not go away with you, it was not at all because I was afraid of being found out by the guards and getting lashed, or of being eaten by sharks or dolphins and becoming a sea-spirit, and it was not from a dread that your seventh escape would fail too and we would be hauled back together.

Papillon! Before you left, I could never have told you this, but I have realized that, even supposing there really is a promised land waiting with open arms to welcome us when we reach the mainland, there is no new life for us. You see, I have come to realize that this world is all a prison, no matter where you go, and that all people without exception are convicts in it.

I have realized that a life spent under the fierce glares of the guards who watch over this "Island of Death", and getting along with all the dangerous ruffians housed in our cell, while raising the 200 pigs I am in charge of, that such a life is no better and no worse than life anywhere else in the world.

빠삐용! 그래서 자네가 찾아서 떠나는 자유도 나에게는 속박으로 보이는 걸세. 이 세상에는 보이거나 보이지 않거나 창살과 쇠사슬이 없는 땅은 없고, 오직 좁으나 넓으나 그 우리 속을 자신의 삶의 영토로 삼고 여러 모양의 밧줄을 자신의 연모로 변질시킬 자유만이 있단 말일세.

빠삐용! 이것을 알고 난 나는 자네마저 홀로 보내고 이렇듯 외로운 걸세.

* 드레퓌스의 벤취; 앙리 샤리에르의 탈옥 수기《빠삐용》에 나오는 <죽음의 섬> 벼랑에 있는 벤취로 유태 출신 프랑스 육군 대위로 반역죄에 몰려 이 섬에 유형流刑되었다가 12년 만에 복권된 드레퓌스의 이름을 딴 것임.
* 짱; 주인공 빠삐용의 탈출을 돕고도 <죽음의 섬>에 그대로 남는 중국계 도형수徒刑囚 이름.

Papillon! Therefore the freedom that you are leaving here in search of looks to me just like shackles. I feel that in this world there is no land without barred windows and chains, visible or invisible, there is only that freedom which we make our life's domain within ourselves and which transforms every kind of bond into our own loving and yearning.

Papillon! Having come to see all this, I let you go off alone, and now I am so very lonely.

In Henri Charrière's "Papillon", "Dreyfus' Bench" is the name given to a bench on the clifftop of the Island of Death, the penal colony. Jean is a Chinese prisoner who befriends the main character but refuses to escape with him.

어느 까치들의 울음

서울시청 옥상.
철망 속의 까치들은
먼저 눈이 짓물러갔다.
공중에 자욱한 배기가스 탓도 있지만
자신들의 오늘이 하도 기막혀
마냥 눈물을 흘려서다.

제때마다 뿌려 주는 모이를 쪼으면서도 눈물이 나고
양푼의 물로 목을 축이면서도 눈물이 나고
광장까지 날아 오르내리는 비둘기 떼를 보아도
눈물이 나고
인왕산仁旺山 봉우리나 덕수궁德壽宮 숲을 바라보아도
눈물이 나고
꼬리를 물고 달리는 자동차의 행렬을 보아도 눈물이 나고
거리를 오고가는 사람들의 물결을 보아도 눈물이 나고
이따금 위세를 떨치며 나타나는 나으리를 보아도
눈물이 나고
저녁 때 인조 둥지 속에 웅크리고 들어앉아도
눈물이 나고
밤하늘의 별을 쳐다보아도 눈물이 나고
추억에 잠겨도 눈물이 나고
미래를 떠올려도 눈물이 나고
더구나 이 우리 속에서 낳아 자라고 있는 새끼들을 보면
눈물이 쏟아지고

Weeping of Magpies

On the roof of Seoul City Hall,
magpies in a cage, earlier than others
show running eyes.
Partly on account of the all-pervading exhaust fumes,
but mainly they weep
because their present life is so awful.

Pecking at the regularly scattered grain, they weep.
Sipping the water in a bowl, they weep.
Watching the pigeons flying in the square, they weep.
Looking across to the distant hills,
seeing the trees in the near-by park, they weep.
Watching the cars lined up nose-to-tail, they weep.
Beholding the people coming and going, they weep.
Seeing the highest authority at times appear, they weep.
Huddled at night in artificial nests, they weep.
Looking up by night at the stars in the sky,
they weep.
Recalling the past, they weep.
Imagining the future, they weep.
And if they consider the chicks
that hatch and grow up in their cage,
the tears pour down.

서울시청 옥상,
철망 속의 까치들은
먼저 눈이 짓물러갔다.

On the roof of Seoul City Hall,
magpies in a cage, earlier than others,
show running eyes.

월남기행 越南紀行

나는 어디서 날아온 지 모르는
메시지 한 장을 풀려고
무진 애만 쓰다 돌아왔다.

꾸몽 고개 야자수 그늘에서
봉다워 바닷가에서
아니 사이공의 아오자이 낭자娘子와
마주 앉아서도
오직 그것만을 풀려고
애를 태다 돌아왔다.

아마 그것은 베트콩이 뿌린
전단傳單인지 모른다.

아마 그것은 나트랑 고아원서 만난
월남越南 소년의 장난인지 모른다.

아마 그것은 어느 특무기관特務機關이
나의 사상을 시험하기 위한
조작造作인지 모른다.

Back from Vietnam

After vain efforts to decipher this message,
a single page that fluttered down from somewhere,
I have returned.

In the shade of palm trees at Kumong Pass,
beside the sea at Vongtau,
even sitting with aodai-clad bargirls
in Saigon,
I strove to decipher it, in vain;
I have returned.

It might be propaganda
dropped by the Vietcong. I am not sure.

Or a trick by a Vietnamese child
I met at Natrang orphanage. I am not sure.

Maybe it is a ploy of some secret service,
to test my way of thinking.
I am not sure.

아마 그것은 로마 교황의
평화를 호소하는
포스터인지 모른다.

아니 그것은 우리의 어느 용사가
남겨 놓고 간 유서인지도 모른다.

마치 그것은
흐르는 눈물 모양을 하고 있었다.

마치 그것은
고랑쇠 같은 모양을 하고 있었다.

마치 그것은
포탄으로 뻥 뚫린
구멍 모양을 하고 있었다.

마치 그것은
사지四肢를 잃은
해골 모양을 하고 있었다.

아니 그것은
눈감지 못한
원혼冤魂의 모습을 하고 있었다.

It might be a poster
of the Pope's appeal for peace.
I am not sure.

Or perhaps, rather, it may be a last will and testament
left by one of our Korean heroes.
I am not sure.

You see, it was
in the form of a falling tear.

You see, it was
in the form of prison fetters.

You see, it was
in the form of a hole
pierced by a falling shell.

You see, it was
in the form
of a limbless skeleton.

Or rather, it was
in the shape of a bitter spirit
unable to find rest.

그런데 그것은
월남越南 이야기인 것도 같고

그런데 그것은
나 개인의 문제인 것도 같고

그런데 그것은
우리 민족과 관련된 것도 같고

아니 그것은 보다 더
인류와 세계에 향한
강렬한 암시暗示 같기도 하였다.

내가 그것으로 말미암아
오직 느낀 것이 있다면
나란 인간이
아니 인류가
아직도 깜깜하다는 것뿐이다.

나는 그 메시지를
풀다 풀다 못하여
이제 고국에 돌아와서까지
이렇듯 광고한다.

Yet it seemed
to be something to do with Vietnam.

Yet it also seemed
to be something concerning me in particular.

Yet it also seemed
to concern my fellow-countrymen.

But it seemed mainly
to be a strong suggestion
aimed at all the peoples of the world.

And the only thing that I have felt
thanks to it
is that I as an individual,
that indeed the whole of humanity,
we are all still utterly ignorant. Only that.

So now, still unable
to really decipher the message,
since I have managed to return,
I publish it like this.

백지白紙 위에
선혈鮮血로 그려진
의문부疑問符
　?
그게 무엇이겠느냐?

On a sheet of white paper
traced in red blood
a question-mark:
   ?
What can it mean?

귀가歸家

제미니 6호를 타고
랑데부를 마친 후
돌아오는 참엔

저녁 때, 들에서
목동들이 소를 타고
버들피리 불며
마을로 들어서듯

비프스테이크를 한 입 덜 먹고
몸무게를 줄여
팔 포키트에 숨겨 가지고 간
하모니카를 꺼내
풍팡풍팡 불면서
아내와 어린 것이 기다리는
지구로 내렸다.

* 이 소재는 연전 제미니 6호의 우주 비행사 쉴러 대령이 한국에 왔을 때 기자 인터뷰에서 술회한 사실이다.

Homeward Journey

On board Gemini 6,
the rendez-vous completed,
on the way back down,

just as in the evening
farmers return homeward
riding on oxen
and playing willow flutes,

eating one mouthful less of steak
to reduce his weight
then pulling out the harmonica
hidden in an arm pocket
and making music, oomp-pa-pa,
eager to be home with wife and kids,
he sailed back down earthwards.

펜의 명銘

한 방울의 이슬이 지각地殼을 뚫어
샘으로 솟는
그 청렬淸洌한 정열로
펜을 들자.

밀림에다 불을 붙이고
원야原野를 갈아 새 밭을 일구는
그 푸른 꿈으로
펜을 들자.

천척千尺 탄갱炭坑 속을 뚫어 나가는
광부의 비지땀으로
펜을 들자.

심장수술心臟手術에 임한 외과의外科醫 메스의
그 과학성과 조심스러움으로
펜을 들자.

The Pen

As a drop of dew penetrates the ground
then issues as a springing source,
with that same limpid energy
let us wield the pen.

As men set fire to dense forests
then till the wild and create new fields,
with that same fertile vision
let us wield the pen.

With all the arduous sweat of the miner
piercing rock a thousand feet below
let us wield the pen.

With all the precision and care
of the surgeon's scalpel in an open heart
let us wield the pen.

태산泰山 마루 백설白雪같이 빛나는 이성理性으로
격전장激戰場 전초前哨 수색대의 기민機敏으로
쇠굴레를 입으로 끊는 노예奴隷의
선택과 결단으로
시지프스의 좌절과 절망을 씹어가며

짓밟힌 어린 잡초雜草에도 눈물짓는
사랑을 안고
백결百結의 가난한 회심會心 속에서
펜을 들자.

With reasoned thought
bright as the snow on high mountains,
with the dexterity of soldiers
checking front-line positions,
with the slave's resolve and determination
as he breaks his irons with his bare teeth,
overcoming discouragement and despair
like Sisyphus,

vested with a love that weeps even to see
a new-sprung weed trampled on,
with the spiritual poverty of a Paek-Kyol*,
let us wield the pen.

---

* *Paek Kyol, literally "Hundred Patches" was a famous scholar renowned for his great poverty and integrity.*

제4부

신령한 새싹
Spirit-filled Buds

무소부재無所不在

아지랑이 낀 연당蓮塘에
꿈나비 살포시 내려앉듯
그 고요로 계십니까.

비 나리는 무주공산無主空山
어둑히 진 유수幽邃 속에
심오深奧하게 계십니까.

산사山寺 뜰 파초芭蕉 그늘에
한 포기 채송화모양
애련哀憐스레 계십니까.

휘영청 걸린 달 아래
장독대가 지은 그림자이듯
쓸쓸하게 계십니까.

청산이 연장連嶂하여
병풍처럼 둘렸는데
높이 솟은 설봉雪峰인 듯
어느 절정絶頂에 계십니까.

In all Places

Are you within such stillness
as when, above a shimmering pond,
a dreamlike butterfly gently descends?

Are you obscurely there
in the desolate hills under rain,
their secluded places wrapped in darkness?

Are you the compassion in temple courts
where a flowering plantain's leaves
shelter a single rose-moss flower?

Are you found forlorn
beneath the bright hanging moon,
like shadows cast by a rooftop terrace?

Are you in some such height
as where chains of blue-tinged peaks
rise like screens around,
but above towers one snow-bright?

일월日月을 조응照應하여
세월 없이 흐르는 장강長江이듯
유연悠然하게 계십니까.

상강霜降 아침
나목裸木 가지에 펼쳐 있는
청렬淸洌 안에 계십니까.

석양이 비낀
황금 들판에 넘실거리는
풍요 속에 계십니까.

삼동三冬에 뒤져 놓은
번열煩熱 식은 대지大地같이
태초太初의 침묵沈默을 안고 계십니까.

태풍 휘몰아 오고
해일海溢 일며
천둥 번개치듯
엄위嚴威로서 계십니까.

Are you in such perfect composure
as the long river timelessly flowing,
reflecting the sun and the moon?

Are you in the transparent frost
that unfolds on chill autumn mornings,
coating the naked branches?

Are you within that abundance
that undulates in the fields,
gold in the setting sun's slanting rays?

Are you too reduced to original silence,
like the soil ravaged by long winter's cold,
all fever spent?

Are you in such solemn power
as when the typhoon surges
and tidal waves race,
with clashes of lightning and thunder?

허허창창虛虛蒼蒼 하늘과 바다가 맞닿은
무애無涯도 넘어
아득히 계십니까.

칠색七色의 무지개 위에나
성좌星座를 보석자리 삼아
동천東天의 일출日出마냥
휘황스레 계십니까.

이화梨花, 도화桃花 방창方暢한데
지저귀는 저 새들과
옥류玉流에서 노니는 고기 떼들의
생래生來의 즐거움으로 계십니까.

풀잎 뜯어 새김하며
먼 산 한 번, 구름 한 번 바라보는
산양山羊의 무심으로 계십니까.

저고리 섶을 연 젖무덤에 달려서
어미를 쳐다보는 아기의 눈빛 같은
무염無染 속에 계십니까.

Are you as far removed
as the blending of vast blue immensity,
sea and sky made one
beyond all boundlessness?

Are you resplendent
as daybreak in the eastern sky,
high above the sevenfold rainbow's gleam,
like constellations' jewelled thrones?

Are you within the inborn joy
of swarms of fish flashing in jade-green streams
and the birds that chirp
while plum and peach delicately bloom?

Are you in the impassibility of a sheep
that nibbles grass then chews the cud,
looking up now at a cloud, now at a hill?

Are you in the innocence shining
in the eyes of a child gazing at its mother
and clasping her breast through an open blouse?

저 신선도神仙圖
흰 수염 드리운 그윽한 미소로
굽어 살피고 계십니까.

이렇듯 형상形相으론 섬기지 못하고
붓 안 닿는 여백같이
시공時空을 채워 계심이여!

무소부재無所不在, 무소부재無所不在의
하느님!

Are you looking down on us
with the profound white-bearded smile
of drawings of Taoist Mountain Wizards?

You who fill all space and time,
whom I cannot serve under any such forms
but who resemble the white spaces in pictures
where the brush did not pass!

In no place confined,
by nothing defined,
everywhere present,
Lord God of all!

요한*에게

너, 아둔한 친구 요한아!
가령 네가 설날 아침의 햇발 같은 눈부신 시를 써서 온 세상에 빛난다 해도 너의 안에 온전한 기쁨이 없다는 것을 아직도 깨우치지 못하느냐.

너, 아둔한 친구 요한아!
가령 네가 미스 월드를 아내로 삼고 보료를 깐 안방과 만 권萬卷의 서書가 구비된 사랑에 살며 세 때 산해진미山海珍味로 구복口腹을 채운다 해도 너의 안에 온전한 기쁨이 없다는 것을 아직도 깨우치지 못하느냐.

너, 아둔한 친구 요한아!
가령 네가 남보다 뛰어나는 건강을 가졌거나 천만인을 누르는 권세를 쥐었거나 화성火星을 날으는 재주를 지녔다 해도 너의 안에 온전한 기쁨이 없다는 것을 아직도 깨우치지 못하느냐.

너, 아둔한 친구 요한아!
가령 네가 너의 아들 딸들의 지극한 효를 보고 그 손주 놈들의 재롱에 취한다 해도 너의 안에 온전한 기쁨이 없다는 것을 아직도 깨우치지 못하느냐.

To John*

John! My slow-witted friend!
Have you still not understood that perfect joy would not be in you, even if having written poems bright as the sun on a New Year's morning you enjoyed world-wide fame?

John! My slow-witted friend!
Have you still not understood that perfect joy would not be in you, even if you were to marry Miss World and live in rooms spread with rich cushions and supplied with ten thousand books, sitting down three times a day to delicious meals?

John! My slow-witted friend!
Have you still not understood that perfect joy would not be in you, even if your health were far better than anyone else's, or if you held power over tens of millions of subjects, or if you were able to fly to Mars?

John! My slow-witted friend!
Have you still not understood that perfect joy would not be in you, even if you were adored and revered by your sons and daughters, while you lived entranced by the cute antics of all your little grandchildren?

너, 영혼의 문둥이 요한아!

만일 네가 네 안에 참된 기쁨을 누리자면 너의 오늘날 삶의 모든 것이 신비神秘의 샘임을 깨달아 그 과분함을 감사히 여길 때 이루어지리니 그래서 일찍 너의 형제 아씨시 프란치스코는

"하느님께서 내게 주신 은혜를 거두어 도둑들에게 주셨더라면 하느님은 진정 감사를 받으실 것을!"

하고 갈파喝破하였더니라.

* 요한은 필자의 세복명.

Ah, John! You old leper soul!

Why, if you want to find true joy welling up within you, well, you may realize one day that everything in your present life is a source of mystery and you may come to feel gratitude for so many undeserved gifts; therefore your brother, Francis of Assisi, exclaimed:

"If the Lord were to take from me all the grace he has bestowed, and give it to thieves instead, he would receive my sincerest thanks!"

*The poet's baptizmal name is John.

그 분이 홀로서 가듯

홀로서 가야만 한다.
저 2천 년 전 로마의 지배 아래
사두가이와 바리사이들의 수모를 받으며
그 분이 홀로서 가듯
나 또한 홀로서 가야만 한다.

악의 무성한 꽃밭 속에서
진리가 귀찮고 슬프더라도
나 혼자의 무력無力에 지치고
번번이 패배의 쓴 잔을 마시더라도
제자들의 배반과 도피 속에서
백성들의 비웃음과 돌팔매를 맞으며
그 분이 십자가의 길을 홀로서 가듯
나 또한 홀로서 가야만 한다.

정의正義는 마침내 이기고 영원한 것이요,
달게 받는 고통은 값진 것이요,
우리의 바람과 사랑이 헛되지 않음을 믿고서
아무런 영웅적英雄的 기색도 없이
아니, 볼꼴없고 병신스런 모습을 하고
그 분이 부활復活의 길을 홀로서 가듯
나 또한 홀로서 가야만 한다.

As He Walked Alone

I must walk alone.
As he walked alone
two thousand years ago under Roman rule,
to the insults of Scribes and Pharisees,
so I too must walk alone.

Among luxuriant gardens of evil,
although the truth is sad and hard,
although I often taste the bitter cup of failure,
exhausted in lonely helplessness,
just as he walked alone along the Way of the Cross,
betrayed, abandoned by the disciples,
with people mocking and throwing stones,
so I too must walk alone.

Trusting that justice will triumph, eternal,
trusting that suffering accepted has value,
trusting that our love and hope are not vain,
not putting on heroic airs,
with nothing to show but a cripple's grace,
just as he walked alone on the way of Resurrection,
so I too must walk alone.

성탄절聖誕節 고음苦吟

구유 위의 당신을 첫 조배朝拜하던
목동들의 순박한 기쁨과
그 외양간의 단란마저 깨진
교회당敎會堂,

당신 왕국의 건설을 두려워하는
헤로데와 그 군사들이
이 밤도 당신의 새 순을 자르기에
눈 뒤집혀 지새우는 크리스마스,

복음福音을 쇼 윈도의 구슬옷처럼
조명에 따라 변색시키는
당신의 제자들과
그 열광의 무리와
바리사이 파派들에게 오늘도 에워싸인
당신,

자캐오*처럼 나무에 올라
한 마리 까마귀 영혼이 우짖는다.
"나와 우리의 이 주박呪縛에
눈을 돌려 주소서!"

* 자캐오; 신약성서에 나오는 착한 세리稅吏 난쟁이여서 예수를 만나려고 나
  무 위에 올라가 외쳐댐.

Christmas lament

Ah, the venerable Church!
With none of the simple joy of those shepherds
who came first to worship around your crib!
With nothing left of the peace of your stable.

Fearing the coming of your kingdom,
tonight too Herod and his henchmen keep watch,
ready to lop off your young shoots,
keeping Christmas with glaring eyes.

Your disciples, changing the color of the Gospel
like a beaded dress displayed in a shop window,
the color varying with the lighting,
with the enthusiastic mob,
and the Pharisees, today too, crowd around
you;

and like Zaccaeus perched in a tree,
one crow-like soul cries:
"On me and on all held in cursed bondage
turn, oh turn your eyes!"

부활송復活頌

죽어 썩은 것 같던
매화의 옛 등걸에
승리의 화관花冠인듯
꽃이 눈부시다.

당신 안에 생명을 둔 만물이
저렇듯 죽어도 죽지 않고
또다시 소생蘇生하고 변신變身함을 보느니
당신이 몸소 부활로 증거한
우리의 부활이야 의심할 바 있으랴!

당신과 우리의 부활이 있으므로
진리眞理는 있는 것이며
당신과 우리의 부활이 있으므로
정의正義는 이기는 것이며
당신과 우리의 부활이 있으므로
달게 받는 고통은 값진 것이며
당신과 우리의 부활이 있으므로
우리의 믿음과 바람과 사랑은 헛되지 않으며
당신과 우리의 부활이 있으므로
우리의 삶은 허무虛無의 수렁이 아니다.

Easter Hymn

On an old plum tree stump,
seemingly dead and rotten,
like a garland of victory
flowers gleam, dazzling.

Rooted in you, even in death
all things remain alive;
we see them reborn, transfigured.
How could we doubt our Resurrection
since by your own you have given us proof?

Since there is your Resurrection and ours,
   Truth exists;
since there is your Resurrection and ours,
   Justice triumphs;
since there is your Resurrection and ours,
   suffering accepted has value;
since there is your Resurrection and ours,
   our faith, hope, love, are not in vain;
since there is your Resurrection and ours,
   our lives are not an empty abyss.

봄의 행진이 아롱진
지구 어느 변두리에서
나는 우리의 부활로써 성취될
그날의 누리를 그리며
황홀에 취해 있다.

In this lost corner of the earth,
dappled by the spreading spring,
as I imagine that Day's world,
made perfect by our Resurrection,
I am overwhelmed in rapture.

성모상聖母像 앞에서

은방울 꽃에서는
성모聖母의 냄새가 난다.

지구의地球儀 위에 또아리를 틀고 엎드려
당신의 그 고운 맨발에 깔린 뱀은
괴롭기커녕 눈을 가늘게 뜨고
고개를 갸우뚱 졸고 있다.

푸른 보리 비린내를 풍기고
지나가는 봄바람이
당신의 흰 옷자락과 남빛 띠를
살짝 날리고 있고
흰 수건을 쓰고 우러르는
당신의 눈빛엔 한恨이 담겨 있다.

이 나라 청자青瓷의 하늘을 넘어
저 깊은 허무虛無의 바다도 넘어서
당신의 명주明紬 가슴에다
칠고七苦*의 생채기를 내고 간
아들, 예수의 나라가
예서도 보이는가?

Before the Virgin's Statue

Your sweetness, Holy Mother,
comes rising from the lily of the valley!

Held down by your pretty bare feet,
coiled flat on top of the earthly globe,
not at all ill at ease, with eyes half shut
the serpent dozes and shrugs.

Shedding as it passes by
a strong smell of fresh green barley
slyly the spring breeze stirs your skirts
and the deep blue belt with your white veil;
your eyes that scan the skies
hold a gleam of vague resentment.

Beyond this nation's celadon skies,
beyond deep gulfs of vast nothingness,
can you glimpse from here
the Kingdom of Jesus your son
who went away, leaving in your silken breast
the wounds of the Seven Sorrows?

루르드* 바위 그늘에
무릎을 꿇어 합장合掌한
오월五月의 오후!
만물萬物의 숨결이 고르다.

* 칠고七苦 ; 가톨릭에서는 마리아의 모성母性으로서의 고통을 크게 일곱 가지
로 든다.
* 루르드 ; 프랑스의 지명, 마리아가 나타난 곳으로 그 바위 굴의 모형을 따
서 우리 성단 안에도 성모상을 안치함.

This May afternoon,
as I kneel with hands joined
in the shadow of the cliff at Lourdes,
all things are breathing regularly.

신령한 새싹

그다지 모질던 회오리바람이 자고
나의 안에는 신령한 새싹이 움텄다.

겨울 아카시아모양 메마른
앙상한 나의 오관五官에
이 어쩐 싱그러움이냐?

어둠으로 감싸여 있던 만물萬物들이
저마다 총총한 별이 되어 반짝이고
그물코처럼 엉키고 설킨 사리事理들이
타래실처럼 술술 풀린다.

이제 나에게는 나고 스러지는 것이
하나도 가엾지가 않고
모두가 영원의 한 모습일 뿐이다.

때를 넘기면 배가 고프고
신경통으로 사지四肢가 쑤시기는
매한가지지만

나의 안에는 신령한 새싹이 움터
영원의 동산에다 피울
새 꽃을 마련하고 있다.

Spirit-filled Buds

The pitiless whirlwinds have died down,
spirit-filled buds are opening in me.

What then is this freshness
touching my gaunt senses
that were dry as winter acacia trees?

All things, once plunged in darkness,
turn into stars and begin to shine;
until now locked in a tangled mesh,
my ideas flow free like thread from a skein.

Now there is nothing sad for me
about being born only to die;
all is just one aspect of eternity.

I still feel hungry if a meal is delayed,
my limbs still have rheumatic twinges,
nothing has changed, but within me

Spirit-filled buds have begun to grow,
preparing to bloom with new flowers
once in Eternity's land.

신령한 소유所有

나는 이제사 탕아蕩兒가 아버지 품에
되돌아온 심회心懷로
세상 만물을 바라본다.

저 창 밖으로 보이는
6월의 젖빛 하늘도
싱그러운 신록新綠 위에 튀는 햇발도
지절대며 날으는 참새 떼들도
베란다 화분에 흐느러진 페추니아도
새롭고 놀랍고 신기하기 그지없다.

한편 아파트 거실을 휘저으며
나불대며 씩씩거리는 손주놈도
돋보기를 쓰고 베갯모 수를 놓는 아내도
앞 행길을 제각기의 모습으로 오가는 이웃도
새삼 사랑스럽고 미쁘고 소중하다.

오오 곳간의 재물과는 비할 바 없는
신령하고 무한량한 소유!
정녕, 하늘에 계신 아버지 것이
모두 다 내 것이로구나.

Spirit-filled Wealth

Feeling today like the Prodigal Son
just arrived back in his father's arms,
I observe the world and all it contains.

June's milky sky glimpsed through a window,
the sunlight dancing over fresh green leaves,
clusters of sparrows that scatter, chirping,
full-blown petunias in pots on verandas,
all strike me as infinitely new,
astonishing and miraculous.

My grandchild, rushing round the living-room
chattering away, my wife, her glasses on,
embroidering a pillow,
and the various neighbors,
coming and going below,
all are extremely lovable, trustworthy, significant.

Oh, spirit-filled, immeasurable wealth!
Not to be compared with storeroom riches!
Truly, all that belongs to my Father in Heaven,
all, all is mine!

말씀의 실상實相

영혼의 눈에 끼었던
무명無明의 백태가 벗겨지며
나를 에워싼 만유일체萬有一切가
말씀임을 깨닫습니다.

노상 무심히 보아 오던
손가락이 열 개인 것도
이적異蹟에나 접하듯
새삼 놀라웁고

창 밖 울타리 한 구석
새로 피는 개나리꽃도
부활復活의 시범示範을 보듯
사뭇 황홀합니다.

창창蒼蒼한 우주, 허막虛漠의 바다에
모래알보다도 작은 내가
말씀의 신령神靈한 그 은혜로
이렇게 오물거리고 있음을
상상도 아니요, 상징도 아닌
실상實相으로 깨닫습니다.

The True Appearance of the Word

As the cataract of ignorance falls
from off the eyesight of my soul,
I realize that all this huge Creation
round about me is the Word.

The hitherto quite unattended fact
that these familiar fingers number ten,
like the encounter with some miracle,
suddenly astonishes me

and the newly-opened forsythia flowers
in one corner of the hedge beyond my window
entrance me utterly,
like seeing a model of Resurrection.

Smaller than a grain of sand
in the oceanic vastness of the cosmos,
I realize that this my muttering,
by a mysterious grace of the Word,
is no imagined thing, no mere sign,
but Reality itself.

나자렛 예수

나자렛 예수!
당신은 과연 어떤 분인가?

마굿간 구유에서 태어나
강도들과 함께 십자가에 못박혀 죽은
기구망측한 운명의 소유자,

집도 절도 없이 떠돌아 다니며
상놈들과 창녀들과 부역자들과
원수로 여기는 딴 고장치들과
어울리며 먹고 마시기를 즐긴 당신,

가난한 사람들에게
굶주린 사람들에게
우는 사람들에게
의로운 일을 하다 미움을 사고
욕을 먹고, 쫓기고
누명을 쓰는 사람들에게
"행복된 사람은 바로 당신들"이라고
"하느님 나라는 바로 당신들 차지"라고
엄청난 소리를 한 당신,

Jesus of Nazareth

Jesus of Nazareth!
Who are you really?

Born in a stable's manger,
dying nailed to a cross with thieves,
the unlucky possessor of an absurd destiny.

Wandering around, without house or home,
you kept company with low class people,
with prostitutes and rebels,
with louts from other regions
normally considered enemies;
you enjoyed eating and drinking with them.

To the poor,
to the hungry,
to those in tears,
to those despised for their just deeds,
insulted, driven out, and dishonored
for having practiced what is right,
you dared to proclaim:
"You, you are the blessed!
Yours, yours is the Kingdom of God!"

소경을 보게 하고
귀머거리를 듣게 하고
앉은뱅이를 걷게 하고
문둥이를 말짱히 낫게 하고
죽은 사람을 살려 내고도

스스로의 말대로
온 세상의 미움을 사고
욕을 먹고, 쫓기다가
마침내 반역자란 누명을 쓰고
볼꼴 없이 죽어 간 철저한 실패자,

내가 탯줄에서 떨어지자 맺어져
나의 삶의 바탕이 되고, 길이 되고
때로는 멀리하고 싶고 귀찮게 여겨지고,
때로는 좌절과 절망까지를 안겨 주고
때로는 너무나 익숙하면서도
생판 낯설어 보이는 당신,

당신의 참모습은 과연 어떤 것인가?

You gave sight to the blind,
you opened the deaf man's ears,
you made the cripple walk,
you completely healed the leper's sores,
you brought the dead back to life,

as you yourself said,
heaped with the whole world's hatred,
insulted and driven out,
finally labelled a traitor
and dying without any show,
you are the ultimate failure

and to me, united with you from my mother's womb,
you are the very ground of my being, the way
from which, at times, I incline to stray,
finding it a nuisance,
at times a cause of discouragement, despair;
at times, although extremely familiar,
you look like an absolute stranger.

So what on earth are you really like?

당신은 사상가가 아니었다.
당신은 도덕가가 아니었다.
당신은 현세의 경륜가가 아니었다.
아니 당신은 종교의 창시자도 아니었다.

그래서 당신은 어떤 지식을 가르치지 않았다.
당신은 어떤 규범을 가르치지 않았다.
당신은 어떤 사회 혁신운동을 일으키지 않았다.
또한 당신은 어떤 해탈을 가르치지도 않았다.

한편 당신은 어느 누구의
과거 공적이 있고 없고를 따지지 않았고
당신은 어느 누구의
과거 죄악의 많고 적음을 따지지 않았고
당신은 실로 이 세상 모든 사람의
생각이나 말을 뒤엎고
"고생하며 무거운 짐을 지고
허덕이는 사람은
다 나에게로 오라,
내가 편히 쉬게 하리라"고
고통받는 인류의 해방을 선포하고

You were not a thinker,
you were not a moralist,
you were not one of this world's statesmen,
and you were not the founder of a religion.

Therefore, you did not teach any kind of learning,
you did not teach any kind of rules,
you did not launch any kind of social reform movement,
you did not teach detachment from this world.
You did not compute
anyone's past merit, or lack of it,
you did not compute
anyone's past sins, whether many or few.
Really, you overturned the thoughts and words
of everyone in the world:
"Come to me, all you
who are toiling and struggling along
under heavy burdens,
I will give you rest!"
To suffering humanity
you proclaimed liberation,

다만, 하느님이 우리의 아버지시요,
그지없는 사랑 그 자체이시니
우리는 어린애처럼 그 품에 들어서
우리도 아버지가 하시듯 서로를 용서하며
우리도 아버지가 하시듯 다함 없이 사랑할 때

우리의 삶에 영원한 행복이 깃들고
그것이 곧 "하느님의 나라"라고 가르치고
그 사랑의 진실을 목숨 바쳐 실천하고
그 사랑의 불멸을 부활로서 증거하였다.

and you taught that God is our Father,
that he is Love itself, infinite,
that when, nestling like children in his breast,
we forgive as our Father forgives,
and love as our father loves,

then eternal bliss dwells in our lives,
and that, you taught, is called "the Kingdom of God"
and having practiced at the cost of your life
the sincerity of such loving,
you bore witness by your Resurrection
to that Love's imperishability.

제5부

초생달 꽃밭
Garden by Moonlight

영춘무 迎春舞

옛 등걸 매화가
흰 고깔을 쓰고
학鶴춤을 추고 있다.

밋밋한 소나무도
양팔에 푸른 파라솔을 들고
왈츠를 춘다.

수양버들 가지는 자진가락
앙상한 아카시아도
빈 어깨를 절쑥대고
대숲은 팔굽과 다리를 서로 스치며
스텝을 밟는다.

길 언저리 소복한 양지마다
잡초 어린것들도 벌써 나와
하늘거리고

땅 밑 창구멍으로 내다만 보던
씨랑 뿌리랑 벌레랑 개구리도
봄의 단장을 하느라고
무대 뒤 분장실扮裝室 같다.

Springtime Dances

The old plum tree stump,
wimpled in white,
is dancing the dance of the crane.

The towering pine trees,
extending green parasols in either hand,
are performing a waltz.

Weeping willows sway in rhythms free,
bony acacias
rock leafless shoulders,
while bamboos rubbing arms and legs
step it out together.

Along the wayside where snow meets the sun
tiny blades of grass, already sprouting,
gently sway.

Seeds, roots, insects, frogs,
that had only been peeping from underground windows
now put on their springtime best,
like actors in backstage dressing rooms.

바람 속의 봄도
이제는 맨살로 살랑댄다.

Now the breath of spring in the breeze
comes gently brushing the naked flesh.

봄 빨래

보리밭 옆구리
수양버드나무가
강에다 머리를 감는다.

햇발이 물 밑에서
금모래로 아른거리며
머뭇거리고 흐른다.

땅 속에서 갓 나온
청개구리들모양 엎드려
마을 새댁과 처녀들이
봄 빨래가 한창이다.

철석 철석,
딱딱, 쭈룩 쭈룩,
마치 흰떡을 치고
주무르듯 하며

짹 짹, 종알 종알,
캬들 캬들, 캑 캑,
힝힝, 해해들이다.

Spring Washing

Along the edge of a barley field
weeping willow trees
dip their tresses in a stream.

Sunbeams beneath the water,
turned to golden grains of sand, dance
then pause, then flow again.

Hunched like toads
new crawled from the ground,
the village women and girls
attack the springtime washing.

Slip-slop slip-slop,
tacka-tacka-tacka, slosh-slosh,
they beat away
as if pounding out the rice-cake paste.

Chick-check, chick-chock,
yick-yeck, yick-yock,
heh-heh, hee-hee! The tongues wag away:

말띠 딸을 낳고 시아버지에게
눈치가 뵈던 얘기,
극성맞은 시어머니 얘기,
시큰둥스러운 학생 올케의 얘기,
휴가 왔다 간 남편 얘기,
○○당黨 망나니 얘기,

아롱진 저 정경 속엔
청상과수의 수틀처럼
아직도 서러운 사정들이
얼룩져 있다.

Here's a baby girl born in the year of the horse!
The father-in-law's not too pleased about that!
And here's a mother-in-law too strict by half,
or a cheeky student for a sister-in-law,
but there a husband's gone back after leave,
and as for the gangsters of a certain political party,

In this pleasant scene
there still remain shadows of personal pain,
like stains in the embroideries
made by young widows.

봄 국화

매머드 아파트 창가에
귤상자 조각을 막고
50원어치 흙을 사다
10원어치 씨를 뿌린 봄 국화가
노랑
빨강
분홍
연두
흰빛 등
꽃술을 달고 있다.

인공人工 속에 홀로 핀 자연의 숨결!

봄 아침의 햇살이 찾아들다
눈부시어 돌아서고

맞은편 채 3층에서 분홍 이불을
혓바닥같이 드리우던 댄서 아가씨가
눈을 가늘게 뜨고 건너다 보고
윗 6층에서 재즈곡을 듣던 대학생이
부스스한 머리의 비듬을 털면서
내려다보고

Spring Chrysanthemums

At the window of a large flat,
in an old orange-box
with a scrap of soil
and a packet of seeds sprinkled,
spring chrysanthemums
yellow
red
pink
turquoise
white
are spreading their petals.

Nature blossoming alone in an artificial world!

Scarcely arrived, the spring-morning sunshine
dazzles, then slips away.

At the third floor opposite, a pink blanket
waves like a tongue while the owner,
a dancer, squints across;
above, on the sixth floor, a student is listening to jazz,
brushing the dandruff from bushy hair
and staring down.

아래층 은행수위銀行守衛 집 마누라가 수건을 쓰고
총채로 방석을 내털다가
쳐다보고

옆집 정년퇴직한 홀 늙은이가
어항에 물을 갈아 주다
고개를 외로 돌려 보고

왼편 집 꼬마 형제가
소꿉 세간을 늘어 놓다
돌아다보고

한길에 방울을 흔들며 지나가던
두부장수가
고개를 치켜 쳐다보고
손수레를 밀고 지나가던
빙과장수도
땀을 씻으며 쳐다보고

이 방 앳된 안주인은
손조리로 물을 주며
방금, 혓바닥을 몇 번씩이나 깨물리며
떠밀어 출근시킨
서방님 생각을 어이없이 하면서
생글생글 웃는다.

On the ground floor a bank-guard's wife,
her perm in a towel
glances up as she fiercely beats cushions,

And the unmarried pensioner next door,
changing the water in his goldfish-bowl,
stops and looks sideways

while the two kid brothers to the left
stop playing at housekeeping
and turn to look.

In the street a bean-curd seller,
ringing a hand-bell as he passes,
stops and looks up
and the ice-cream man,
pushing his cart along,
looks up too, wiping his brow

while the newly-married housewife
watering her flowers
cannot help thinking of her husband
whom she has just pushed off to work,
after a good number of tongue-bites,
and very slightly she smiles.

하일서경 夏日叙景

1. 아침

산과 마을과 들이
푸르른 비늘로 뒤덮여
눈부신데

광목처럼 희게 깔린 농로農路 위에
도시에선 약 광고에서나 보는
그런 건장한 사내들이
벌써 새벽 논물을 대고
돌아온다.

2. 낮

'이쁜이'가 점심함지를
이고 나서면
'삽살이'도 뒤따른다.

사내들은 막걸리 한 사발과
밥 한 그릇과
단잠 한 숨에
거뜬해져서 논밭에 들면
해오리 한 쌍이
끼익 소리를 내며
하늘로 날은다.

Scenes of a Summer's Day

1. Morning

Mountains, villages and fields,
all decked with scales of green,
dazzle the eyes,

along long cotton-white paths fit like those
in advertisements for health products,
out since dawn
irrigating the rice-fields,
are returning homewards.

2. Noontide

A jolly lass sets out, bearing the workers' lunch
in a basket on her head,
a hairy dog trotting behind her.

Refreshed by a scoopful of makkoli,
a bowl of rice,
a moment's snooze,
the men go back to the rice fields,
while a pair of white herons
fly across the sky
with a creaking sound.

3. 저녁

저녁 어스름 속에
소를 몰아
지게 지고 돌아온다.

굴뚝 연기와
사립문이 정답다.

태고太古로부터
산과 마을과 들이
제자리에 있듯이

나라의 진저리나는
북새통에도
이 원경原景에만은
안정이 있다.

3. Evening

Through the evening twilight,
driving a cow,
with a frame on their backs, they return.

The smoke from kitchen fires,
the brushwood gate, offer warm welcome.

As from time immemorial,
hills, villages, fields,
all are unchangingly here,

and even in this land's present chaos
this primordial scene
is in itself enough
to restore serenity.

실향失鄕 바다

남빛 바다에 뜬
하늘을 타고 헤엄치다
푸성귀마냥 퍼래져서
찰싹이는 파도이랑을 넘어
베폭처럼 펼쳐진 모래밭에 올라가
지글거리는 태양을 깔고 덮고 뒹굴다가
해당화 울타리 너머
제물 차일遮日의 솔숲으로 들어서
그 푸른 그늘 아래
왕성한 식욕食慾을 채운다.
나의 실향失鄕, 나의 실락원失樂園,
원산元山 송도원松濤園!

파란 스커트를 걸친
명주빛 젖무덤에다
흰 타올을 두른
용광로 가슴이
황금빛 정열을 퍼부어
천지天地가 눈부시다.
명사십리明沙十里.

친구여, 서양 친구*여!
그대는 지중해, 열사熱砂의 바다를
삶의 피안彼岸으로 삼는가?

Seaside in a Lost Homeland

First, you bathe in the blue vault of the sky
as it dips itself in the radiant sea,
then, once become pale as green vegetables,
you plough through the thunderous surf
and climb the sandy beach, spread like sackcloth,
and wallow stretched out in the scorching sun;
then, passing a fringe of flowering shrubs,
you enter the green shelter of a pine grove
and there, in its green shade,
you satisfy your healthy appetite.
Ah, my lost homeland! My lost Paradise!
Wonsan! Songdowon!

Above your deep blue skirts,
over your silken breasts
a white towel lies stretched
and your heart vibrates heat,
a golden light as from a furnace,
and the whole universe is glorious.
Miles of bright sand!

My friend, my Western friend!
Do you really think the Mediterranean,
that sea of burning strands,
can be life's ultimate shore?

아닐세, 그 아닐세,
이글이글 태양과 푸른 바다와
흰 파도와 불꽃이 튀는 모새밭만으론
우리가 기리는 해방은 없느니,

이렇게 한번 상상해 봄세!
가령, 저 태평양太平洋 한복판
사방四方 아득히 밀려가고 밀려오는
그 창연悵然과 허막虛漠 앞에서,

가령, 저 아라비아 사막 뙤약볕 아래
타들어오고 숨막히는 갈증 속에서
이 사람! 어찌 삶을 구가謳歌한단 말인가?

그것은 진실로 두려운 노릇일세,
짐짓 우리 본향本鄕 실존實存의 마을엔
솔숲, 내 원산元山 바다와 같은
솔숲을 두어야만 쓰느니
그리고 가끔 죽음과 같은
서늘한 그늘 아래 쉬어야만 하느니
친구여, 서양 친구여!

*'서양 친구'라 함은 대개 알베르 카뮈를 가리킨다.

No, surely not!
It is not just a matter of scorching sun and blue sea,
of white waves and sparkling strands,
for the liberation we desire is not there.

Only imagine for a moment!
In the very centre of the Pacific Ocean,
that immeasurable vastness
surging to and fro in all directions,
endless on every side;

or in the Arabian deserts, beneath a scorching sun
the suffocating tortures of thirst,
tell me, how could we ever celebrate life there?

It is a terrifying thing, you know,
but I have to have in life's primordial village
a pine grove as by my Wonsan sea shore;
and at times beneath a death-like cloud of sorrow
I must remain and rest.
My friend, my Western friend[*]!

---

* *The 'Western friend' is Albert Camus.*

달밤

달이 으슥한 우물 안에서
철렁철렁 목욕을 하다
두레박을 타고 올라와
질옹배기로 흘러 들어간다.

이번엔 햇바가지에 담겨
새댁의 검은 머리채 위서부터
보얀 등허리와 볼록한 앞가슴을
미끄러져 내려
빨랫돌 위에 산산이 부서진다.

달로 씻은 육신은 달처럼 희다……

노란 지붕 위에서
내려다보던 고추들이
얼굴을 더욱 붉힌다.

어느 새 중천中天에 다시 올라간
달을 쳐다보고
박덩이가 쩔쩔매며
넝쿨 뒤로 숨는다.

꽃밭에서 이를 바라보던 봉선화가
너무나 재밌어 꽃잎을 떨구며
눈에 이슬을 단다.

Moonlit Evening

As the moon was bathing lazily
in the still waters of a well,
it was caught in the bucket, up it went,
was poured out into a stoneware jar.

Scooped from there in a fresh hollow gourd,
it flowed all down a bride's black hair,
over creamy back and swelling breasts,
down it slipped, and away it went,
splashing into shivers on a washing-stone.

The moon-washed flesh was now white as moon······.

From high up on the straw-pale roof
the pepper-pods look down,
their faces blush redder than ever.

Glancing up at the moon,
now somehow back up on high,
the pumpkins are embarrassed
and shyly creep under their vines.

In the flower-beds the balsam flowers watch it all,
they see and drop petals at so much fun,
moistening their eyes with dewdrops.

초동初冬의 서정抒情

상강霜降

마지막 잎새마저 떨어진
고목古木 가지에
서리 핀 아침이 드맑게 펼쳐 있다.

소년 적 죄그만 가슴의 그리움이던
교리방敎理房 수녀의 흰 이마가
아련히 떠오른다.

청렬淸冽이 결코 설움은 아니련만
내 눈에는 찬 이슬이 맺힌다.

입동立冬

헤식어 가는 햇발이
긴 그림자를 끌고
양지陽地를 찾는다.

대지大地는 번열煩熱을 가시고
본래本來대로 누워 있다.

11월의 일모日暮엔
나의 인생도 회귀回歸에 든다.

Thoughts as Winter Comes

First Frost

Along the branches of old trees,
stripped of every last leaf,
the hoarfrost-flowering morning cleanly spreads.

The ivory brow of the catechism sister,
object of my tiny breast's deepest childhood longing,
creeps into my mind.

Purity is no matter for melancholy, surely,
yet my eyes are moist with a chill dew.

First Day of Winter

Feebly advancing sunbeams
dragging long shadows
seek out the sunny spots.

The earth, with no fever left,
lies in its primitive state.

In this November twilight
my life, too, begins its return.

초설初雪

첫눈을 맞을 양이면
행복한 이에겐 행복이 내려지고
불행한 사람에겐 시름이 안겨진다.

보얗게 드리운 밤 하늘을
헤치고 가노라면
등불의 거리는 고성소古聖所처럼 그윽한데

멀리 어디선가
기항지寄港地 없는 뱃고동 같은 게
쉰 소리로 울려온다.

First Snow

When the first snowfalls come,
blessings descend on the blessed
but anguish seizes the wretched.

As snow drops down pale
from the dark night sky,
the lamplit streets become silent sanctuaries

and from some distant place
a raucous sound echoes,
like the call of a boat which has lost its port.

겨울 거리에서

붉은 벽돌 빌딩에 낡은 현수막이
실의失意같이 드리운 겨울 일모日暮,
앉은뱅이 철책鐵柵 앞 포도鋪道 위에
시멘트 지대紙袋 조각을 사장沙場 삼아
남생이 새끼 몇 마리가
옹기종기 모여 있다.

나목裸木의 가로수처럼 앙상한 사내가
보얗게 먼지를 쓰고 서서
거미손으로 실을 잡아당길 양이면
남생이는 쪼르륵 쪼르륵 달려나가고
쪼르륵 쪼르륵 달려나가단
종이 사장沙場에서 떨어지고

드르륵 드륵 드르륵
은행의 철문鐵門이 내려지면
눈앞엔 어둠의 장막이 드리우고
눈도 돌리지 않는 사람의 파도가 밀려
선창船艙 같은 혼잡 속에서
버스는 다가오고 떠나가고

딛고 선 아스팔트 밑에
연탄빛 여윈 청계천淸溪川이 지나가듯
사내의 주린 창자 속에서도

In a Winter Street

The winter twilight hangs despairingly
like the tattered banner on the red brick building,
while on the sidewalk before a crippled fence,
with strips of cement sacks in place of a sandy beach,
a few baby tortoises
lie heaped together.

A salesman stands gaunt as the roadside trees,
veiled in whitish dust,
and when his spidery hand pulls the thread it holds,
the baby tortoises scrabble, scatter,
scrabble, scrabble, scatter,
and fall off their paper shore.

Rattle, rattle, crash!
As the shutters slam down in front of the bank
a veil of darkness descends before the eyes;
a wave of people presses on, unseeing,
and with a dock-side uproar
buses screech in and away.

As the coal-black waters of a meager stream
flow unseen beneath the asphalt where he stands,
so too in the hungry innards of the salesman,

쪼르륵 쪼르륵 남생이가 달려나가고
달려나가단 떨어지고

외론 섬 등대마냥 켜 보는 칸델라 불에
종이 조각 보는 어안魚眼렌즈 속의 해저海底,
아니면 갈가마귀 새끼 떼들이
내려앉은 무덤,

이 처량한 정경情景에선
죽은 전우의 송장이라도 다가와
손을 잡으면 반가와 눈물지리.

scrabble, scrabble, the turtles run
and as they run they fall.

The lamp shines dim like a lighthouse on a desert
island,
the scraps of paper seem a sea-bed
viewed through a fish-eye lens, or a tomb on which a
flock of jackdaws has settled.

In this desolate scene, suppose the corpse
of some dead wartime companion should come up
and clasp his hand, he would weep for joy.

제6부

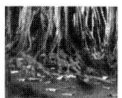

연작시
Poem Cycles

모과木瓜* 옹두리에도 사연이
— 청소년 시절의 회상기

1

고삐 풴
거품 뿜고
침 흘리는 소.

네 살, 나에게 비로소 있음이
예루살렘 여인네가 내민 수건에
피땀으로 인印쳐진 사형수死刑囚의
바로 그런 소 얼굴.

묵화墨畵의 산에 미끄럼대로 걸린
진노을 황토黃土 길
앞 달구지에 얹혀
밧줄로 묶인 이조李朝 장롱을 싣고
뒤따르던 그 소 얼굴에서
나의 새순은 움트며 흐느꼈다.

* 모과 木瓜 ; 모과나무의 열매, 한자漢字로는 木瓜로 표기함.

Even the Knots on Quince Trees
—Memories of Youth

1

A bridled,
foaming,
drooling cow.

Aged four, my first revelation of really existing
found in a face like that printed by blood and sweat
on a cloth held out by a Jerusalem woman to a man
on his way to execution: the face of a cow.

The yellow, twilit path slid up over a mountainside,
calligraphic in black and white;
I sat perched on the leading cart,
an old cupboard lay tied in the wagon behind,
as my first buds of knowledge unfolded
in the face of the cow plodding behind, I wept.

2

외사촌 누나의 수틀이
눈에 익은 때문일까.

나의 죄그만 가슴이
그리움에 미어 바라보고 있었다.

강이 교리방敎理房 수녀의 흰 고깔 밑
보얀 얼굴을 크게 번지면서
북간도행北間島行 열차의 기적汽笛을 내며
흘러가고 있는 것을…….

내가 해의 적막寂寞한
뒤통수를 본 것도
이 때다.

2

Could it have been
from long familiarity
with my cousin's embroidery frame?

My little breast
tortured with longings, I gazed up.

Over the wimple and creamy face
of the catechism-class sister,
whistling like a train leaving for the North,
a river was spreading wide······.

I saw
the desolate back of the sun
that day, too.

3

소신학생小神學生이
정월 초하루 아침
백설白雪 차림의 황후폐하皇后陛下 사진을
신문서 도려 갖고
후들후들 변소로 들어섰다.

창세기의 배암이 온몸을 조여
모독冒瀆의 정열을 고름 빼듯 한 후
3년 머물던 수도원修道院을 등졌다.

그리고 나는 주의자主義者가 되었다.

3

In Minor Seminary,
early one New Year's Day,
having cut out from the newspaper a picture
of Her Imperial Majesty all dressed in white,
I rushed straight to the toilets.

Having done like the serpent in Genesis,
who, squirming his whole body, expelled
like pus a blasphemous passion,
I turned my back on that monastery
in which I had spent three years.

And I became a follower of isms.

4

출발이 도망이었다.

밤의 현해탄玄海灘을
다다미 한 장에 뒤친다.

올빼미 눈이 번득이는 선실船室은
출구 없는 갱도坑道,
발동소리가 심장을 난타亂打한다.

역사의 쇠사슬을 찬 젊은이는
망토를 제끼며 일어나 앉아
이름 모를 짐승이 되어
치를 떤다.

스승도 없는 갈릴레아!

암흑의 파도를 타고
머리 푼 윤심덕이
손짓한다.

4

I began by running away.

On the night ferry to Japan,
tossing on a single tatami space,

the cabin with its owl's eye
is a miniature tunnel with no way out,
and the roar of the engines tortures my heart.

one young man,
fettered in chains of history,
throwing aside his coat and sitting up,
turns into a nameless beast
and grinds his teeth.

Galilee with no Master!

Riding the waves of darkness,
Yun Shim-Dok* with hair untressed in grief
hails me.

---

*Yun Shim-Dok was a hero of the Korean anti-Japanese resistance movement.

5

울먹이도록 화창한 적도敵都의 봄,
미사 경본*과
빈보모노가타리*를
옆구리에 겹쳐 끼고
종일 향방없이 헤맨다.

돌이키질 못할 역사로 흘러가는
아라카와*를 지나
기타센주* 어느 목로판으로 들어섰다.
요보일고용 들 틈에 끼어
도부로쿠를 들이킨다.

쾌지나 칭칭 나네!
누가 혀나, 누가 혀나,
그 등불을 누가 혀나
캄캄한 이 밤중에
우리 등불을 누가 혀나
쾌지나 칭칭 나네!

5

In this enemy town, on a spring day so harmonious
it brings tears to my eyes, with a missal
and a book called "Wretchedness"
wedged under my arm,
all day long I wander aimlessly.

Crossing the Aragawa,
which flows towards its irreversible history,
I enter a bar in Kitashenshu
and sit squeezed between Korean laborers
to swallow down my toburoko.

Kwejina chingching naneh!
Who will light, who will light
this lamp, who will light?
In the midst of this dark night
who will light our lamp?
Kwejina chingching naneh!

스무 살, 첫 입댄 술에
귀로歸路는 하늘도 거리도
사람도
반 고흐의 〈별 있는 밤〉 풍경.

* 빈보모노가타리; 원제목 『貧乏物語』, 일본 사회주의 경제학자의 저서.
* 아라카와; 동경 만彎으로 흐르는 강.
* 기타센주; 동경 해변의 빈민촌.
* 도부로쿠; 일본 술의 한 종류.

Twenty years old, my first taste of drink:
on the way home, sky and streets
and people too
looked like Van Gogh's "Starry Night".

6

그때
라 로쉬코우* 공公과의 해후는
나의 안에 태풍을 몰아왔다.

선善한 열망熱望의 첫 꽃망울들은
삽시에 무참히도 스러지고
어둠으로 덮인 나의 내부엔
서로 물어뜯고 으르렁거리는
이면수二面獸의 탄생을 보았다.

자기증오自己憎惡의 밧줄이
각각으로 숨통을 조여오고
자연의 침묵은 공포로 변했으며
모든 타자他者는 지옥地獄*이요
인생은 더할 바 없는 최악의 세계…….

하숙방 다다미에 누워
나는 신의 장례식을
날마다 지냈으며

6

At that time
the encounter with La Rochefoucauld
aroused a typhoon within me.

The early buds of eager desire to do good
vanished brutally, in a flash,
and, darkness-wrapped within,
I saw two-headed monsters come to life,
that tore at each other, roaring.

Moment by moment cords of self-hatred
tightened around my throat;
the silence of nature changed into horror,
other people became "hell"
and human existence a world of utter evil……

Stretched out on my boarding-house tatami floor,
I celebrated daily
funerals of God

길상사吉祥寺* 연못가에 앉아
차라투스트라가
초인超人의 성城에 오르는
그 황홀을 꿈꿨다.

* 라 로쉬코우; 프랑스의 모럴리스트(1613~1680).
* 타자他者는 지옥地獄; 사르트르의 말.
* 길상사吉祥寺; 도쿄 교외공원 지명.

and sitting beside a pond in Kitsijoji Park,
I imagined the rapture
of a Zarathustra
climbing up to the stronghold of the Superman.

7

카페 '에트랑제'의
유미짱은
백계白系 러시안의 피섞인
낭자娘子.

처음에는 그녀에게
누이동생이 되어 주기를
졸랐지만 허탕.

어느 자정子正 가까이
위트카 몇 잔을 들이켜고
앵도 입술을 덮쳤을 때
그녀, 그 때만은
"오빠! 이런 짓 못써요!"

나의 사랑 행적은
줄곧 저런 허구와
불일치!
그리고 측은의 결말結末.

7

In the coffee-shop 'Etranger'
was Yumi,
a Eurasia girl
with White Russian blood.

At first I pestered her
to become my little sister,
but with no success.

One evening, near midnight,
after several glasses of vodka,
when I suddenly fell on her cherry lips,
just that once she exclaimed,
"No acting like that, brother!"

The course of my love :
constantly such falsehoods,
no unity!
And a miserable conclusion.

30년이 지난 이즈음도
꿈의 도원桃源에서
유미짱과 번번이
안타까운 봉별逢別.

나는 애정의 임포텐스.

Thirty years later, even now,
in the Shangri-la of dreams
I always feel anxious
about my encounter with Yumi.

Affection in me impotent!

8

두이노의 비가悲歌는
나의 무성한 가지에
범신汎神의 눈을 트게 하였다.

나의 성명性命은 아침의 풀이슬
이제까지 모습만으로 있던
만물만상萬物萬象이
안으로부터 빛을 낳고
또 나날이 죽어 가고 있었다.

무상無常의 흐느낌이
찰랑거리던 어느 날
나의 안에는 노래의 샘이
흐르기 시작하였다.

살이 잎새되고
뼈가 줄기되어
붉은 피로 꽃 한 떨기
피우는 그 날까지
목숨이여!

나의 첫 시詩 첫 구절이다.

* 두이노의 비가悲歌; R. M. 릴케의 시

8

On my thickly growing branches
the Duino Elegies
brought out buds of pantheism.

My human life: a morning dewfall on the grass,
all things existing,
hitherto mere appearance,
bringing forth light from within
and, day by day, dying.

One day, as the tears
of impermanence were brimming full,
a fountain of song
began to rise within me.

Until that day when my flesh becomes leaves,
my bones stalks,
and when from my scarlet blood
a bouquet of flowers shall rise,
ah, my life!

The first phrase of my first poem.

9

골고타의 모자母子 이름을
혀 마르도록 부르며
되부르며 숨져갔다.

이승과 저승이
고통의 쇠사슬로 이어지는
그런 죽음,

촛불을 혀고 연도煉禱가 울려 퍼지는
시신屍身 앞에서
저의 삶 위에 빚어졌던
고통! 그것의 씨알이 정녕 무엇일까?
무참히도 몰라졌다.

그러나 나의 혈관 속에 이어진
바로 그 숙명의 분류奔流!
단종斷種을 다그쳐 생각하며

흉하게 굳어진 애비에게서
고개를 돌이켰을 때
곡哭이 터져 나왔다.

9

Invoking Golgotha's Mother and Son,
praying so hard it parched his tongue,
still invoking, he died.

Such a death
in which this world and the world beyond
are linked by chains of pain,

With candles burning and prayers for the dead rising,
before that corpse,
molded over my life, such pain!
And born of what seeds?
Not knowing was the worst torment.

But the torrent of that destiny
continued to flow in my veins!
Abruptly thinking to cut off that inheritance,

as I turned my face away
from my hideously stiff father,
I broke into a wail.

10

한동안 나는 노장老莊과 소요逍遙하며
어문語文놀이를 즐겼다.

벗어라 벗어라
네가 벗어라
네가 벗지 않으면
내가 벗으마.
속아라 속아라
네가 속아라
네가 속지 않으면
내가 속으마.

한편 나는 토속신土俗神들과도 사귀며
신명풀이에 미쳤다.

띠띠고 신신고
호랑이 꼬랑이
개구리 대구리
물레에 괴머리
베틀에 쇠꼬리.

10

For a while, frequenting Lao Tzu and Chuang Tzu,
I enjoyed playing with words:

empty, empty,
you must empty,
if you empty me not away,
I'll empty you away.
Play, play,
you must play,
if you play no tricks on me,
I'll play tricks on you.

Then somehow, frequenting folklore gods,
I went crazy exorcising:

belt and shoes,
tiger, tailor,
frogs, clogs,
spinning spindle,
loom and treadle.

초토焦土의 시

1

판잣집 유리딱지에
아이들 얼굴이
불타는 해바라기마냥 걸려 있다.

내려 쪼이던 햇발이 눈부시어 돌아선다.
나도 돌아선다.
울상이 된 그림자 나의 뒤를 따른다.

어느 접어든 골목에서 걸음을 멈춘다.
잿더미가 소복한 울타리에
개나리가 망울졌다.

저기 언덕을 내려 달리는
소녀의 미소엔 앞니가 빠져
죄 하나도 없다.

나는 술 취한 듯 흥그러워진다.
그림자 웃으며 앞장을 선다.

Wasteland Poems

1

Against the window panes of a wretched hovel
children's faces
press like blazing sunflowers.

They turn away, dazzled by the sun's piercing,
and I too turn away;
a moping shadow trudges behind me.

Down an alley chosen at random I pause;
in a hedge half-smothered in ashes
forsythia flowers are budding.

Down the hill a little girl comes running,
smiling a gappy smile with no front teeth,
absolutely blameless.

I cheer up like after a drink
and my shadow goes prancing ahead, grinning.

2

내 가슴 동토凍土 위에
시베리아 찬바람이 살을 에인다.

말라빠져 엉켜 뒹구는 잡초雜草의 밭
쓰레기 구덩이엔
입벌린 깡통, 밑나간 레이션 박스,
찢어진 성조지星條紙, 목 떨어진 유리병,
또 한 구석엔 총 맞은 삽살개 시체,
전차戰車의 이빨자국이 난 밭고랑엔
말라 뻐드러진 괭이의 잔해,
저기 비닐 온상 같은 천막 앞
피묻은 바짓가랑이가 걸린
철망 안을 오가며
양키병정이 획획 휘파람을 불면
김치움 같은 땅 속에서
노랗고 빨갛고 파란
원색原色의 스카프를 걸친 계집애들이
청개구리들처럼 고개를 내민다.

하늘이 갑자기
입에 시꺼먼 거품을 물고
갈가마귀 떼들이 후다닥 날아
찌푸린 산을 넘는데

2

On the frozen ground of my heart
a bitter Siberian wind bites the flesh.

In a field of dry tangled weeds
a garbage dump
of gaping cans, smashed ration-boxes,
pages from an Army newspaper, broken bottles,
and in one corner the cadaver of a hairy dog, shot dead;
along the ridges bitten into the fields by tanks
the dry stiff carcass of a cat;
in front of a tent like a plastic hot-house
behind barbed-wire hung with blood-stained slacks,
coming and going, a yankee soldier;
whenever he whistles, peep-peep,
wretched urchins pop up their heads, like frogs, from
holes in the ground like those where kimchi is kept,
wrapped in colored scarves,
yellow, red and blue.

The sky suddenly
begins to spew black mist
and a cluster of crows flaps off
over the sullen hills.

나의 잔등이 미칠 듯한 이 개선疥癬!
나의 가슴을 치밀어 오르는 이 구토嘔吐!
어느 누구를 향한 것이냐?

This itch in my back that drives me mad,
this rising bile that dilates my breast,
what can it be caused by?

3
— 적군*敵軍墓地 앞에서

오호, 여기 줄지어 누웠는 넋들은
눈도 감지 못하였겠구나.

어제까지 너희의 목숨을 겨눠
방아쇠를 당기던 우리의 그 손으로
썩어 문드러진 살덩이와 뼈를 추려
그래도 양지 바른 두메를 골라
고이 파묻어 떼마저 입혔거니
죽음은 이렇듯 미움보다도 사랑보다도
더욱 신비스러운 것이로다.

이 곳서 나와 너희의 넋들이
돌아가야 할 고향땅은 30리면
가로막히고
무주공산無主空山의 적막만이
천만 근 나의 가슴을 억누르는데

*여기서 적군敵軍은 북한군을 가리킴.

3
—Before a War Cemetery of North Korean dead

Ah, surely they could never close your eyes,
you, souls now resting here in rows?

It was these our hands, that until yesterday
pressed the trigger and took your lives, that
gathered up your broken, rotting bodies, your bones,
chose a secluded mountainside where the sun is right,
and quietly buried them, covered the spot with turf,
for truly death is more mysterious
than hatred or love.

Not far from here the road is blocked,
the homeward road
your souls, like mine, must take,
and the mere silence of the empty, desert hills
weighs on my breast a thousand tons ;

살아서는 너희가 나와
미움으로 맺혔건만
이제는 오히려 너희의
풀지 못한 원한이
나의 바람 속에 깃들어 있도다.

손에 닿을 듯한 봄 하늘에
구름은 무심히도
북으로 흘러가고
어디서 울려오는 포성砲聲 몇 발
나는 그만 이 은원恩怨의 무덤 앞에
목놓아 버린다.

so while in life we were
only united in hate,
now rather the tragic longing
you were not able to allay
dwells within my aspiration.

In the spring sky, nearly close enough to touch,
a cloud indifferently
floats North-ward;
gunfire echoes from afar
and before these tombs of love and hate
all I can do is weep copious tears.

밭 일기 日記

1

밭에서 싹이 난다.
밭에서 잎이 돋는다.
밭에서 꽃이 핀다.
밭에서 열매가 맺는다.

밭에서 우리는
심부름만 한다.

Diary of the Fields

1

In the fields young shoots appear.
In the fields the leaves unfold.
In the fields the flowers bloom.
In the fields the fruits ripen.

In the fields, what can we do?
All we can do is run errands.

2

농부가 소를 몰아
밭을 간다.

막혔던 땅의
숨구멍이 터진다.

얼어붙었던
가슴이 열린다.

봄 하늘이
손에 잡힐 듯하다.

소와 농부가 함께
쳐다본다.

구름이 북으로
흘러간다.

엄매……

가시도 덩굴도
헤치며
갈아나간다.

2

Urging on his ox,
the farmer ploughs his field.

The blocked pores of the ground
burst open.

The frozen lungs
expand again.

The spring sky
seems near enough to touch.

Ox and peasant both
look up at it together.

A cloud
drifts North-wards.

Moooo!

The plowshare bites into the soil,
ripping through
thorns and creepers.

3

서릿발 과질이 서걱거리는 보리밭을
초예醮禮의 3일을 치른 내외가
서로 얼굴을 돌리며 엿보며
밟아 나간다.

움푹 패고 꺼진 두덩엔 흙을 넣어가며
부풀고 들뜨고 홍겨운 마음을 다지듯
채곡채곡 밟아 나간다.

동녘에는 쏟아지는 햇발이 부서져 튀고
남산南山에는 나일론 망사 같은 아지랑이
서향西向 고목古木 가지엔 물동이를 인
빨강 노랑 저고리가 꽃피어 있고
북쪽 마을 노리끼한 볏지붕 굴뚝에선
아침 향연香煙이 일제히 오르고 있다.

눈앞에는 하루살이 떼들이
온실 속 먼지처럼 가물거리고
새들은 호들갑을 떨고 날며 지저귄다.

3

Three days married!
Slyly stealing glances at one another,
the young couple treads down the barley field
which, still frozen, creaks beneath their feet.

Filling the deeply engraved ruts with soil,
as if firming up their swelling, restless hearts,
step by step they tread down the soil.

To the East outpouring sunbeams break through,
to the South a haze dances over the hills
like a nylon veil;
on the branches of an old West-leaning tree
yellow and red jackets blossom,
bearing waterpots on their heads;
in the village huddled to the North
the sweet smoke of morning smoothly rises
from chimneys over yellow thatch.

Like motes of dust in a greenhouse,
swarms of gnats dance before my eyes,
the birds flutter, dive and chirp.

어디선가 햇닭 똥내음 같은
풋내가 풍겨오는데
해토解土의 아침,
세상은 온통 염미艶美를 발산發散한다.

A smell drifts across from somewhere,
like chicken manure,
in the morning when the ground first thaws
the whole world exhales beauty.

4

태양의 용광로鎔鑛爐가 엎질러 쏟아지는
밀림密林 속에다
김치돌만한 부시로
두꺼비 손을 깨면서
생불을 지른다.

충천沖天하는 불길!
삽시에 정글은 불바다다.

로스케나 양키같이
하늘로 치솟은 거목巨木들과
기름가마에 절은 호인胡人녀석의
아름드리 고목古木들과
지난 세월 광기狂氣의 의미도 모르는 채
남북의 군사가 집총執銃을 하듯
빽빽이 늘어선 잡목雜木들과
현실의 증오憎惡와 적개심敵愾心으로

가시가 돋친 덤불과
역사의 악순환惡循還으로 엉키고 설킨

4

In the thick forest
where the furnace-sun pours down heat,
hands like great toads
strike fire from a flint
large as a stone on a storage jar
and, parting, set the fire free.

Flames attack the sky.
In a flash the jungle is a sea of flames.

Towering heavenward, trees
tall as Russians or Yankees,
others with fat trunks
recalling greasy Manchus,
thickly packed bushes
like soldiers of South and North in arms
not understanding the recent madness,
thorn-sharp bushes bristling
with present hates and hostility,

brambles tangled in history's twists,
matted by Destiny's turning wheel,

인업因業의 칡덩굴들과
모든 권력의 숲과
모든 조직의 뿌리까지
그저 이 세기의 사각일대死角一帶가
뇌성벽력雷聲霹靂을 내며
포탄砲彈소리를 내며
송두리째 뒤집히며 불타오른다.

이 무주공산無主空山을 지배하며
제 혼자만의 세상처럼 으르렁대던
호랑이 표범 같은 맹수들도
꽁지에 불을 달고 줄도망을 치며
진창 제 배만을 불리던
곰, 너구리, 멧돼지 족속族屬들은
참호塹壕 같은 불구덩이에 통째로 빠지고
뱀, 여우, 늑대, 삵괭이같이
간사한 무리들은

마지막 순간까지 눈을 해번득이면서
살 구멍을 찾아 요리 뛰고 저리 뛰고
올빼미, 박쥐 같은 날도둑들과
정보망情報網을 드린 거미들,
옴두꺼비, 땅두더쥐, 쥐새끼 같은
첩자와 정탐꾼들,

the forest of all the powers,
down to the roots of every system,
in short, this world's entire dead ground,
with a sound of thunder,
a sound of guns,
is overturned completely and burns.

On the vast deserted mountain heights
where they ruled as undisputed masters,
the tigers, panthers, and other such
flee now with fire at their tails;
bears, badgers and boars,
that had only thought to fill their stomachs,
all fall into blazing trenches and ditches;
snakes, foxes, wolves and wild cats,
all such cunning kind
run hither and thither in search of escape,
their eyes glinting till the end;

owls, bats, and all that steal by night,
the spiders with their information net-works,
the toads, moles, rats, with all such spies and agents,
the bands that eat at every table,
as well as the nests of the birds that sang

요쪽 저쪽 붙어먹던 무리들,
세상 제멋대로 지껄여대던
소음騷音의 새 떼들 둥주리까지
아니, 더러는 무죄無罪한 청개구리마저
탄다.
뻐드러진다.
질식窒息의 매연 속을 뛰며
곤두박질하며 뒹군다.
신음하고 포효咆哮하고 비명을 지른다.
낭자狼藉한 피마저 타들어간다.
지글지글 타들어간다.

넘실거리는 불길의 파도!
타오르는 불길의 산악山岳 속에서
이 강토疆土와 겨레의
모든 주박呪縛이 스러지고
모든 속박束縛이 풀린다.
오오 타라, 타오르라.
한 달도 석 달도 타오르라.
그리고 모든 것이 연기와 재로 사라진 뒤,
피비린내나는 음산陰散마저 가시고 난 뒤,
화장장火葬場의 고요와 산모의 해방감 속에서
출현하는 신령토新領土!
상흔傷痕을 아물리는 새 살처럼
강단强斷된 남북을 합쳐 놓은 원야原野!

and paid no heed to the world's affairs,
yes, even the guiltless little frogs,
all burn.
Stretch dead.
They race around in stifling smoke.
They stumble and roll.
They groan and howl in pain.
Even the blood they shed is consumed,
all crackling, consumed in flames.

A billowing tidal wave of fire!
In this great mountainside blaze
every curse is undone, every bond is unloosed
from off this land, this people.
Oh, then burn on! Burn on!
Burn a whole month! Burn for three!
Once everything has vanished into smoke and ashes,
once the blood-shedding darkness has gone,
in the peace of the pyre,
in the relief of a mother delivered of child,
behold, a new land!

A plain in which North and South shall be one,
now forcibly divided,
united as flesh closes to heal a wound.

거기 노아의 방주方舟에서 갓 나온 듯한
사내와 계집들이
패랭이 고깔을 쓰고
징을 울리고 북을 두드리며
피리를 불고 꽹과리를 치며
나아간다.
땅을 판다.
밭을 일군다.
씨를 뿌린다.
원혼冤魂과 선령善靈들의 귀기鬼氣마저
불살라 버리고 난
이 크낙한 새 밭에
세기世紀의 아침을 맞아
새로 모실 이는
오직 자주自主와 근로勤勞와 화락和樂의
삼위일체三位一體다.

* 이 밭은 어느 화전민火田民의 꿈이다.

There, as if from Noah's Ark,
see women and men advance
wearing plaited bamboo hats,
with sound of gongs, beating drums,
blowing flutes and clashing cymbals
they advance.
They dig the ground.
They cultivate the fields.
They sow the seed.
In this vast new field,
free at last of the shadowy trace
of the resentful dead, now at peace,
celebrating the world's new dawning,
they shall honor anew none but One,
only the Trinity of autonomy, diligence, harmony.

5

나는 아직도 하늘에서 땅에서
또 사람에게서
아무 소리도 듣지 못했노라.

보지도 못했노라.

내 가슴 안에서 피고 스러진
억만億萬의
억만億萬 사연을
단 한 마디 내지도 못했노라.

내 영혼은 본시부터
눈멀어 태었는가?

날이면 날마다
전신의 눈알을 죄다 밝히고
너 하늘을 쳐다보지만
오오 무명無明과 허무虛無의 조우遭遇……

5

I have never heard any voice
be it from heaven, from earth,
or from men.

Neither have I seen any vision.

Within my breast have blossomed and vanished
billions
upon billions of observations,
but I could not express a single word.

Was my soul born, from the very start,
with unseeing eyes?

Day after day, every day
I open wide the eyes of my being
and look up to you, Oh Heavens,
but alas encounter no light, only vast emptiness…….

그리스도 폴*의 강江

1

그저 물이었다.
많은 물이었다.
많은 물이 하염없이
흘러가고 있었다.

흘러가면서 항상
제자리에 있었다.
제자리에 있으면서
순간마다 새로왔다.

새로우면서 과거와
이어져 있었다.
과거와 이어져 있으면서
미래와 이어져 있었다.

과거와 미래가 이어져서
오직 현재 하나였다.
오직 하나인 현재가
여러 가지 얼굴을 하였다.

Christopher's River

1

It was merely water.
It was a great mass of water.
That great mass of water
flowed indifferent on.

Flowing on, it always
stayed in the selfsame place.
Staying in the selfsame place,
it was constantly renewed.

Renewed, although the past
continued steadfast there.
The past continued steadfast,
but the future too was there.

Past and future, thus united,
became one single present.
And that single present moment
showed many faces there.

여러 가지 얼굴을 하고서
여러 가지 소리를 내었다.
여러 가지 소리를 내면서
모든 것에 무심하였다.

무심하면서 괴로워하고
괴로워하면서 무심하고
무심하게 죽어가고
죽어가면서 되살아왔다.

* 그리스도 폴; 가톨릭의 설화 속에 나오는 성인으로 반생半生을 폭력 속에 살다가 어느 강변에서 수도하는 자의 회심回心, 강에서 사람들을 업어 나르는 것을 덕으로 일삼아 마침내 예수의 발현發顯에 접했다고 함.

It showed so many faces,
spoke in many voices.
Speaking many voices,
its heart was indifferent to all.

Always to all indifferent, it suffered,
and suffering it was still indifferent.
Indifferent, one day it died
and dying returned to life.

2

강은 구지레한 마음이 없이
순수한 육신만으로
영원 속의 시간처럼
흐르고 있다.

강은 허접스런 육신이 없이
순수한 마음만으로
시간 속의 영원처럼
흐르고 있다.

강은 마음도 육신도 아닌
허무虛無의 실유實有로
흐르고 있다.

2

The river flows on,
without a filthy heart,
all pure of body,
it flows like time in Eternity.

The river flows on,
without a paltry body,
all pure of heart,
it flows like Eternity in time.

The river flows on,
neither heart nor body,
it flows, an essence of nothingness.

3

강은
과거에 이어져 있으면서
과거에 사로잡히지 않는다.

강은
오늘을 살면서
미래를 산다.

강은
헤아릴 수 없는 집합이면서
단일單一과 평등을 유지한다.

강은
스스로를 거울같이 비워서
모든 것의 제 모습을 비춘다.

강은
어느 때 어느 곳에서나
가장 낮은 자리를 택한다.

강은
그 어떤 폭력이나 굴욕에도

3

The river
continues the past,
is not imprisoned by the past.

The river,
while living today
lives the future too.

The river,
though innumerably collective,
keeps unity and equality.

The river
makes itself an empty mirror
in which all things view themselves.

The river
at all times and in all places
chooses the lowest place.

The river,
unresisting, accepts

무저항無抵抗으로 임하지만
결코 자기를 잃지 않는다.

강은
뭇 생명에게 무조건 베풀고
아예 갚음을 바라지 않는다.

강은
스스로가 스스로를 다스려서
어떤 구속拘束에도 자유롭다.

강은
생성生成과 소멸을 거듭하면서
무상無常 속의 영원을 보여준다.

강은
날마다 팬터마임으로
나에게 여러 가지를 가르친다.

every violence, every humiliation,
and never denies itself.

The river
gives freely to all that lives
and looks for nothing in return.

The river
is its own master,
free despite all bonds.

The river,
caught between generation and extinction,
reveals Eternity within impermanence.

The river
every day in its Pantomime
teaches me many things.

4

눈에 보이는 강의
그 땅 밑으로
또 하나의 깊고 넓은 강이
흐르고 있다.

지층地層의 망사網紗 같은 눈구멍을
세로 가로 뚫으며
실로 캄캄한 어둠 속을
새벽의 날빛처럼 반짝이며
흐르고 있다.

그 백금白金의 강에는
동물이나 식물의 화석들과
더러는 인간의 시신屍身들이
범선帆船들처럼 떠 있고

그 죽은 오브제들이
살아서는 안으로만 품었던
꿈과
사랑과
눈물과

4

Beneath the river bed
that our human eyes can see
there flows another river,
deep and wide.

Piercing downwards and sideways,
forming eyes for the lace-like strata,
sparkling like the dawn
in the deepest darkness,
it flows.

And down that silver river
petrified beasts and plants
float like sailing ships,
with at times a human corpse.

And all around those dead things
float, like a thick mist,
those dreams,
and loves,
and tears,

원한과
기도가
증기蒸氣가 되어
자욱이 서려 있다.

표백表白도 표상表象도 못하는
나의 시심도 이미 함께…….

and grudges,
and prayers,
that alive they kept within.

My poetic thoughts are there too,
the things I can neither express nor represent.

5

오늘도 신비神秘의 샘인 하루를
구정물로 살았다.

오물과 폐수로 찬 나의 암거暗渠 속에서
그 청렬清冽한 수정水精들은
거품을 물고 죽어갔다.

진창 반죽이 된 시간의 무덤!
한 가닥 눈물만이 하수구를 빠져나와
이 또한 연탄빛 강에 합류한다.

일월日月도 제 빛을 잃고
은총의 꽃을 피운 사물들도
이지러진 모습으로 조응照應한다.

나의 현존現存과 그 의미가
저 바다에 흘러들어
영원한 푸름을 되찾을
그 날은 언제일까?

5

I have spent today,
that source of mystery, today,
wallowing in the dirt.

Along the sewers of my soul,
so full of stench and running muck,
the spirits of all purity
have foamed and died.

Tomb of Time turned to a muddy slough!
Just a trickle of tears flows from the drain
and drips into the coal-black stream.

Sun and moon too have lost their shine,
and all those things that once bloomed flowers of grace
reciprocate now with a wilting look.

Ah! When will that day come
when my life and all its meaning
will flow into the distant sea
and recover eternal freshness?

6

강도 날마다 때에 따라
그 표정이 다르다.

어떤 날은
환한 얼굴로
기쁨에 차 있고

어떤 날은
우중충한 얼굴로
우울해 있고

어떤 때는
낯이 핼쑥해서
질려 있고

어떤 때는
낯이 시뻘개서
흥분해 있고

어떤 때는
푹푹 한숨을
쉬고 있고

6

The river, too, day by day,
depending on the moment, puts on a different look.

One day,
beaming brightly,
it is full of joy.

Another day,
glowering,
it lies grim.

At times,
emaciated,
it cowers.

At other times,
crimson-faced,
it gets excited.

Other times,
repeatedly
it sighs.

어떤 날은
훌쩍훌쩍
울고 있다.

강도
내 마음을
닮았는가?

Some days,
sobbing,
it weeps.

Is then the river
so
like my heart?

7

저 산골짜기 이 산골짜기에다
육신肉身의 허물을 벗어
흙 한 줌으로 남겨 놓고
사자死者들이 여기 흐른다.

그래서 강은 뭇 인간의
갈원渴願과 오인嗚咽을 안으로 안고
흐른다.

나도 머지않아 여기를 흘러가며
지금 내 옆에 앉아
낚시를 드리우고 있는 이 막내애의
그 아들이나 아니면 그 손주놈의
무심한 눈빛과 마주치겠지?

그리고 어느 날 이 자리에
또다시 내가 찬미讚美만의 모습으로
앉아 있겠지.

7

Laid along the valleys here and there,
having cast off their carcass of flesh and blood,
nothing now but a handful of earth,
here the ancient dead flow by.

Thus the river clasps to its breast
the desires and sorrows of every person
and flows.

So one day, soon, as I flow by,
shall I not encounter
the unthinking gaze of my youngest child
now fishing here,
of his son or grandson, at least?

And then, one day,
all turned to praise,
I shall sit here again myself!

8

강이 흐른다……

아슴한 옛날이 상여喪輿에 담기고
축열祝列에 아득한 미래가 배듯이
길고 먼 사연의 공백을 안고

강이 흐른다……

동녀童女의 옹달모양 그윽한 샘에
눈물 같은 이슬이 지각地殼을 뚫은
탄생의 신비스런 경이驚異를 품고

강이 흐른다……

아롱진 동경憧憬에 지절대면서
지식의 바위숲을 헤쳐 나오다
천길 벼랑을 내려 구울던
전락轉落의 상흔傷痕을 어루만지며
강이 흐른다……

트여진 대지 위에 백열白熱하던 낭만浪漫과
늪 속에 잠겨 이루던 고독과 기도祈禱,

8

The river flows……

as the bier carries off the days long past,
and the procession is filled with things yet to come,
so, bearing the emptiness of a long, remote story,

the river flows……

bearing the mysterious wonder of the birth
of a tear-like dewdrop passing through the earth,
from a secret source like a virgin's fountain

the river flows……

murmuring all its mottled yearning,
touching the wounds received in falling
against the rocky sides of bottomless chasms,
slipping through the stony labyrinths of knowledge,
the river flows……

tingeing with hope and shame all the
passionate romanticism of the world's vast plains,

오오, 표박漂泊과 동결의 신산辛酸한 기억들을
열망과 수치羞恥로 물들이면서

강이 흐른다……

이제 무심無心한 일월日月의 조응照應 속에서
품에는 어별권속魚鼈眷屬들의 자맥질과
등에는 생노生勞와 환락歡樂의 목주木舟를 얹고
선악善惡과 애증愛憎이 교차交叉하는 다리 밑으로
사랑의 밀어密語와 이별離別의 노래를 들으며
생사生死의 신음呻吟과 원귀寃鬼의 곡성哭聲마저 들으며
일체一切 삶의 율조律調와 합주合奏하면서

강이 흐른다……

샘에서 여울에서 폭포에서 시내에서
억만億萬의 현존現存이 서로 맺고 엉키고 합해져서
낳고 죽어가며 푸른 바다로 흘러들어
새로운 생성生成의 바탕이 되어
곡절曲折로 가득 찬 역사의 대단원大團圓을 지으려고

the solitude and prayer that arise in marshes,
and, ah, the bitter memories of wandering and chill,

the river flows······

now beneath Time's indifferent stare,
bearing in its breast the playfulness of water creatures,
on its back craft of painful labor and of pleasure,
gliding below bridges where good and evil,
love and hatred pass,
hearing whispers of love and songs of parting,
groans of birth, groans of death,
the grief of bitter souls,
making symphony with the rhythms of all that lives,

the river flows······

in sources and rapids, falls and streams,
all the hosts of being join, mingle, unite,
begetting, dying, flowing into the azure sea
to become the origin of new generation
until history at last, in sinuous fullness, perfectly ends,

강이 흐른다……

과거와 미래의 그림자도 없이
무상無常 속에 단일單一한 자아自我를 안고
철석鐵石보다도 굳은 사랑을 안고
영원 속의 순간을 호흡呼吸하면서

강이 흐른다……

또 어느 날 있을 증화蒸化야 아랑곳없이
무아無我의 갈원渴願에 제읍悌泣하면서
염화拈花의 미소를 지으면서

강이 흐른다……

강! 너 허무虛無의 실유實有여.

the river flows……

without any shadow of past or future,
with a constant identity in a world of change,
with a love more solid than any rock,
breathing each present moment in Eternity,

the river flows……

with no concern about imminent evaporation,
weeping with desire for non-being,
smiling at the flower of illusion,

the river flows……

River! Essence of the unbeing Void!

구상 연보

1946 북한 원산元山에서 시집 『응향凝香』에 작품이 수록되어 필화筆禍를 입음
1951 시집 『구상具常』 펴냄
1956 시집 『초토焦土의 시』 펴냄
1960 수상집 『침언부어沈言浮語』 펴냄
1965 희곡 『수치羞恥』 펴냄
1967 연작시 『밭 일기日記』 펴냄
1969 시나리오 『단군檀君』 펴냄
1975 『구상문학선』 펴냄
1976 수상집 『영원 속의 오늘』 펴냄
1977 수필집 『우주인과 하모니카』 펴냄
1978 신앙에세이 『그리스도 폴의 강』 펴냄
1979 묵상집 『나자렛 예수』 펴냄
1980 시집 『말씀의 실상實相』 펴냄
1981 시집 『까마귀』
      시문집 『그 분이 홀로서 가듯』 펴냄
1982 수상집 『실존적 확신을 위하여』 펴냄
1984 자전시집 『모과木瓜 옹두리에도 사연이』
      시선집 『드레퓌스의 벤취에서』 펴냄
1985 수상집 『한 촛불이라도 켜는 것이』
      서간집 『딸 자명紫明에게 보낸 글발』
      『구상연작시집』 펴냄
1986 『구상시전집』
      수상집 『삶의 보람과 기쁨』 펴냄
      파리에서 불어 역 시집 『타버린 땅』 펴냄
1987 시집 『개똥밭』 펴냄
1988 수상집 『시와 삶의 노트』

        시집 『다시 한 번 기회를 주신다면』
        시론집 『현대시창작입문』
        이야기시집 『저런 죽일 놈』 펴냄
1989   런던에서 영역시집 『타버린 땅』
        시화집 『유치찬란』 펴냄
1990   한영대역시집 『신령한 새싹』
        영역시화집 『유치찬란』 펴냄
1991   런던에서 영역연작시집 『밭과 강』
        시선집 『조화造化 속에서』 펴냄

Ku Sang's Literary Career

1946 Poems *Ung-hyang* (Congealed fragrance) not published
1951 Poems *Ku Sang*
1956 Poems *Ch'o-t'o-ui si*(Scorched Earth Poems)
1960 Essays *Ch'im-on-bu-o*
  (Deep Language, Floating Words)
1965 Drama *Su-ch'i* (Shame)
1967 Poem-sequence *Pat'-ilgi* (Diary of the Fields)
1969 Scenario *Tangun*
1975 *Ku Sang mun-hak-son*
  (Ku Sang's Literary Anthology)
1976 Essays *Yong-won sok-ui o-nul*
  (Today within Eternity)
1977 Essays *Woo-ju-in-kwa ha-mo-ni-k'a*
  (Spaceman with Harmonica)
1978 Religious essays *Christo-p'ur-ui kang*
  (Christopher's River)
1979 Meditations *Nazareth Jesu* (Jesus of Nazareth)
1980 Drama *Hwang-jin-i*
  Poems *Mal-ssum-ui sil-sang*
  (The True Appearance of the Word)
1981 Poems *Kka-ma-gui(Crow)*
  Poems/prose *Ku-bun-i hol-lo-so ka-tus*
  (As he walked alone)
1982 Essays *Sil-chon-chok hwak-sin-ul wui-ha-yo*
  (For Practical Assurance)
1984 Autobiographical poems

Mo-kwa Ong-tu-ri-ei-do sa-yon-i
(Even the Knots on Quince Trees Tell Tales)
Selected poems *Dreyfus-ui Bench-ei-so*
(From Dreyfus' Bench)

1985 Essays *Han Ch'os-pul-i-ra-do k'yo-nun kos-i*
(To light at least a candle)
Letters *Ttal Cha-myong-ei-gei po-nen kul-bal*
(Notes to my daughter Cha-myong)
Poem-sequence *Ku Sang yon-chak-si-chip*
(Ku Sang's poem-sequences)
(2 60-poem cycles, "Christopher's River" and "Diary of the Fields")

1986 Anthology *Ku Sang si-son-chip*
(Ku Sang's Anthology)
Essays *Salm-ui po-ram-kwa ki-ppum*
(Life's Reward and Joy)
Translation into French by Roger Leverrier of the selected poems contained in *Dreyfus-ui Bench-ei-so* (1984) under the title *Terre Brûlée*
(Paris. Thesaurus)

1987 Poems *Kae-ttong-pat'* (Dog-shit Fields)

1988 Essays *Si-wa salm-ui no-t'u*
(Notes on Poetry and Life)
Poems *Ta-si han-bon ki-hoi-rul chu-sin-da-myon*
(If you give me another chance)
Poetic theory *Hyun-dae-si ch'ang-chak ip-mun*
(Introduction to the writing of Modern Poetry)
Conversational poems *Cho-ron chuk-il nom*
(That Wretch)

1989 Translation into English by Brother Anthony of the selected poems contained in *Dreyfus-ui*

Bench-ei-so (1984) under the title *Wastelands of Fire* (London. Forest Books)
Poems *Yu-ch'i-ch'an-ran* (Infant Splendor) illustrated with paintings by Chung Kwang

1990 Translation into English by Brother Anthony of the poems contained in *Yu-ch'i-ch'an-ran* (1989) under the title *Infant Splendor* (Seoul, Korea. Sam-seong)

1991 Translation into English by Brother Anthony of 100 of the poems contained in *Ku Sang yon-chak-si-chip* (1985) under the title *River and Fields : A Korean Century* (London. Forest Books)

『한국문학 영역총서』를 펴내며

　한국문학을 본격적으로 번역하여 해외에 소개하는 일이 필요함을 우리는 오래 전부터 절실히 느껴 왔다. 그러나 좋은 번역을 만나기는 좋은 창작품을 만나는 것 못지 않게 어렵다. 운이 좋아서 좋은 번역이 있을 경우에는 또한 출판의 기회를 얻기가 쉽지 않다. 서구의 유수한 출판사들은 시장성을 앞세워 지명도가 높지 않은 한국의 문학작품을 출판하기를 꺼린다. 한국문학의 지명도가 높아지려면 먼저 훌륭하게 번역된 작품들이 세계적인 명성이 있는 출판사에서 출판이 되어 널리 보급이 되어야 하는데, 설혹 훌륭한 번역이 있다 하더라도 이 작품들이 해외에서 출판될 기회가 극히 제한되어 있어서, 지명도를 높일 길이 막막해지는 악순환을 거듭하는 것이 현실이다. 이런 현실을 타개하는 길은 좋은 작품을 제대로 번역하여 우리 손으로 책답게 출판하여 세계의 독자들에게 내놓는 데서 찾을 수밖에 없다. 이런 일을 하기 위해 도서출판 답게에서 "한국문학 영역총서"를 세상에 내놓는다.

　"답게" 영역총서는 한영 대역판으로 출판되며, 이 총서는 광범위한 독자층을 위하여 만들어진 것이다. 무엇보다도 이 총서를 통해 해외의 많은 문학 독자들이 한국문학을 알게 되기를 희망한다. 이 총서는 또한 국내에서 한국학을 공부하거나 영어로 번역된 한국 작품을 필요로 하는 영어 사용권의 모든 사람들과 한국문학의 전문적인 번역자들을 위한 것이기도 하다. 전문 번역인들은 동료 번역자들의 작업을 자신들의 것과 비교함으로써 보다 나은 새로운 번역 방법을 모색할 수 있을 것이다. 고급한 영어를 배우기를 원하는 한국의 독자들도 대역판으로 출간되는 이 총서를 읽음으로써, 언어가 어떻게 문학적으로 신비롭게 또 절묘하게 쓰이는지를 깨닫는 등 많은 것을 얻을 수 있을 것이다.

아무리 말쑥하게 잘 만들어진 책이라도 그 내용이 신통치 않으면 결코 책다운 책일 수 없다는 자명한 이유에서, "답게" 영역총서는 좋은 작품을 골라 최선의 질로 번역한 책만을 출판할 것이다. 또한 새로운 번역자의 발굴과 격려가 이 총서 발간의 목적 가운데 하나이다. "답게" 출판사가 발행하는 이 총서가 한국문학 번역의 중요성을 다시 한 번 일깨우고, 문학 작품의 번역이라는 불가능한 꿈을 가능하게 하려는 번역자들의 노력에 보탬이 되기를 바란다. 이런 시도가 여러 가지로 유용하고 또 도전적인 것이 될 때, 더 나아가서는 잘 번역된 한국 작품의 전세계적인 출판 작업이 이루어지는 단초를 마련할 수 있을 때, 이 선구적인 계획은 진정으로 성공적인 것이 될 것이다.

김 영 무 (서울대 영문과 교수)

Series Editor's Afterword

Extensive translation of Korean literature for the foreign readers has for many years been felt a pressing need. But to fall upon a good translation is much harder than to discern a good original work. If we are fortunate enough to secure a good translation, it is often very difficult to get it published abroad.

The major publishers of the western world are not yet prepared to run the risk of publishing works of relatively unknown Korean literature. Yet if Korean literature is to achieve worldwide fame, it first of all needs to be well translated, and then put into circulation throughout the world by those very publishers which are so reluctant to publish even good translations of Korean literature. It is a vicious circle : no publication without fame but no fame without publication. To save the situation, we should perhaps try to make available to readers abroad choice translations we ourselves have published in editions of high quality. The DapGae English Translations of Korean Literature series has been launched with this aim.

Each volume of the DapGae series will be a bilingual edition. We expect a wide-ranging audience for the series. It is our primary hope that it will help introduce many foreign readers to the world of Korean literature. The series is especially intended to serve English-speaking students enrolled in Korean studies programs and all who need translations of Korean literature, as well as those who may wish to compare their own translations with the translations of fellow translators in order to find new and better ways of translating. Korean readers studying advanced English can also benefit from reading these bilingual editions : the experience may help them to recognize the mystery of true mastery of the literary use of language.

However well designed a book may be, it cannot properly serve its purpose if the contents are mediocre. For that reason, the DapGae series will strive to introduce to the readers of the world the best translations of the finest works of Korean literature. One of the objectives of the series is to find and encourage new talents in English translation. We hope that the DapGae English Translations of Korean Literature series will serve in some small way to refocus attention upon the importance of translating Korean literature into good English and to make possible the impossible dream of literary translation. This pioneering project will be a true success not only if it proves useful and challenging but also if it paves the way for the publication of fine translations of Korean literature on a worldwide scale.

Young-Moo Kim
Department of English
Seoul National University

저자와
협의하여
인지 생략

초토의 시

지은이 | 강영계
펴낸이 | 一庚 張少任
펴낸곳 | 돌산 답게

초판 발행 | 2000년 5월 20일
초판 2쇄 | 2004년 3월 20일

주   소 | 137-834 서울시 서초구 방배4동 829-22호
          원빌딩 201호
등   록 | 1990년 2월 28일, 제 21-140호
전   화 | 편집 02)591-8267 · 영업 02)537-0464, 02)596-0464
팩   스 | 02)594-0464

홈페이지 : www.dapgae.co.kr
e-mail : dapgae@chollian.net

ISBN 89-7574-131-1 02810

나답게 · 우리답게 · 책답게

ⓒ 2000, 구 상

＊ 잘못된 책은 바꾸어 드립니다.